Joseph Georgines

A description of the present state of Samos, Nicaria, Patmos and Mount Athos

Translated by one that knew the author in Constantinople

Joseph Georgines

A description of the present state of Samos, Nicaria, Patmos and Mount Athos
Translated by one that knew the author in Constantinople

ISBN/EAN: 9783742897152

Manufactured in Europe, USA, Canada, Australia, Japa

Cover: Foto ©ninafisch / pixelio.de

Manufactured and distributed by brebook publishing software (www.brebook.com)

Joseph Georgines

A description of the present state of Samos, Nicaria, Patmos and Mount Athos

A DESCRIPTION
OF
The Present State
OF
SAMOS, NICARIA, PATMOS,
and Mount ATHOS.

By *Joseph Georgirenes*,
Arch-Bishop of SAMOS.
Now living in *London*.

*Translated by one that knew the
Author in* Constantinople.

*Dum licet, & vultum servat fortuna benignum,
Romæ laudetur* Samos, *&* Chios, *&* Rhodos *absens.*
Hor. l. 1. Epist. 11.

July 14. 1677.
Licensed,
                         W. Jane.

LONDON,
Printed by *W. G.* and sold by *Moses Pitt*,
at the *Angel* in St. *Paul's* Church-yard. 1678.

TO THE
MOST HIGH PRINCE
Of Royal Birth,
JAMES,
DUKE of York, &c.

JOSEPH GEORGIRENES
Of SAMOS,
The least of Arch-Bishops, offers his most Humble Reverence.

Most High Born PRINCE,

THey that aspire to the Attainment of Wisdom, do not content themselves with the Accurate Search of sublime objects, but also condescend to enquire into lower matters. In like manner, the renowned *Britains* do not confine their contemplations to their own homes, or to

The Epistle Dedicatory.

their neighbour Nations; but enlarge their prospect unto the most remote Countries, and with a piercing Eye, diligently pursue the exact discovery of their state and condition. To which purpose, many persons of honour, and of curiosity, have importun'd me to give some description of the Coasts of *Ionia*, and the *Ægean* Islands; and to declare the present Condition of those great objects of Pity and Protection, the *Greeks*, now under the cruel Tyranny of the Wicked and Barbarous *Hagarens*. The desire I had to gratifie their learned curiosity, whose Judgements I had reason highly to esteem, prevail'd with me to undertake a Description of some Isles of the *Archipelago*, namely, *Samos*, *Nicaria*, *Patmos*, and Mount *Athos*, now called *The Holy Mount*. But because this Work may seem to want that Elegance, or depth of learning, requisite for a Book that must appear upon the Stage of *England*; it stands in need of shelter and protection. Which

lity of flying to the Shadow of your Royal Highness's Patronage, to escape the scorchings of Contempt, and with all humble Reverence, to shelter it under the umbrage of your Royal Highness's propitious Name. And I most humbly offer it; not as a thing of any merit; but as a manifestation of my *devoir* and gratitude; for those great Obligations, which I, and in me all the *Greek* Nation has received. I therefore most humbly beseech your Highness, that as you have thought me worthy of your Bounty, so to continue the same favourable aspect, in accepting this small demonstration of my Gratitude, and by your gracious Patronage, to secure it from their censure, who are not so forward to imitate our well intended pains, as to expose our defects. For which undeserved Favour, we can make Retribution only in our daily Prayers to Almighty God for your Highness's Health and Prosperity in this World, and Eternal Happiness in the World to come.

THE
EPISTLE
TO THE
READER

THe *habitable Earth, by Divine disposal, bestow'd upon the Children of Men, is but one great Island.* And those *Four eminent Parts of it which divide the whole among them, not by equal portions; but by the casual intervention of Seas, are not totally separated one from another; but make one perpetual Continent.* Africa *is joyn'd to* Asia, *by no very small neck of Land betwixt the Mediterranean and the Red Sea: And is no more an Island properly so call'd, than* Peloponnesus. Europe *and* Asia *are joyn'd above the Lake of* Mæotis *with a large space of ground betwixt the Hyperborean Ocean, and that Lake.* And Asia *is joyned to* America, *by the Streights of* Aniam

To the Reader.

Anian *in all probability.* There has nothing yet been discover'd to the contrary, and the great Absurdities that attend the peopling of it are no way so easily solv'd. Besides this Main Continent which is mounted above the Face of the Waters in one entire continuation of parts, there are many lesser Islands, entirely surrounded by the Sea, and divided from all other ground. And all these are but smaller Sisters to that great product of Nature, the Main Continent, not differing from it in kind, but in bulk and size. Whether they owe their birth to the general Deluge, or date their antiquity from the day of the Creation, the Scripture is silent, and so am I. The Opinion of several Islands being rent from the Main Continent, by the violent Incursion of Seas, has been more forwardly embrac'd, than convincingly prov'd, and owes more to Poetical Fancy, than to any solid Foundations of Philosophy. However, tertain it is, that many Islands are of later Antiquity than either the Creation, or the Flood, as on the contrary, many have either

subsided

To the Reader.

subsided, or been over-whelm'd.

The same Earthquake does sometimes produce both effects; and the same time brings Birth to one, and Burial to another. But these are the irregular miscarriages of nature, labouring under a Convulsion Fit, and teach us what may be, not what must be; what nature may sometimes suffer, not what she always doth. As for the whole Globe of Earth and Water, the admirable intermixture of them both for use and beauty, doth highly bespeak the Wisdome of the Maker, and doth no less merit our contemplation, than the Canopy of Heaven. And that the rather, because the inferiour world doth more neerly approach our Senses, and affords us clearer notice of their state and condition. Among all the associate Collection of Islands, that by reason of their mutual vicinity, pass under one common name, there are none more remarkable than those of the Ægean Sea, or the Archipelago. These were so eminent in the days of the Prophets of the Old Testament, that from them all the Western parts of the

To the Reader.

the then known World that was planted principally by the Sons of Japhet, went under the common name of the Isles of the Gentiles, and the Islands of Chittim. The Phœnicians, the first eminent Navigators since the Flood, and the first Planters of Learning and Civility, as well as Colonies, along the shores of the Mediterranean and Atlantick Seas, began their discoveries in these Islands: And there they have left such visible Footsteps of their first Plantation, that the names they bear to this day are most of them of Phœnician Extraction. The Colonies planted in these Islands by the Phœnicians, gave beginning to all those Arts and Sciences for which the Greeks were afterwards so famous, and their Language been held in such admiration to this day. The Æthiopick Islands are known all by Greek names; but they are as far inferiour to the Cyclades in renown, as they are in number, having neither been the Scene of Actions recorded by such Immortal pens, nor the native Soil of persons so eminent for Arts and Arms.

The

To the Reader.

The conceit of Elysium, or such a future happiness as the Heathens dream't of, was thought fit by their Poets to be fix'd upon some remote Islands, therefore call'd the Blessed, or Fortunate Islands. The Hesperides and Canaries have been Competitors for the Title, and our modern searchers into Brittish Antiquity do strain hard to make the Cassiterides, or the Scilly and Man, and Anglesey, put in for a claim. But the Poets have been more accurate in maintaining the Character of an earthly Paradise, and describing a felicity of state beyond that of a Platonick, or Utopian Commonwealth, than in directing us by any rules of Geography, where it is to be found. And as they have left it indifferent to the Reader to fix the Local Situation of such Islands where they will, so they have left it impossible to any Reader to find such a place in the whole World. Indeed it is the high prerogative of great and lasting Wits to affix an esteem and veneration upon those places they make the Stage of their Stories, be they true or false. But

To the Reader.

But in this point of credit, the Islands of the Archipelago *do far surpass any other in the World.* And this is true, not only of the licentious and extravagant Fables of their Romantick Mythologie; *but also in the graver and more creditable Records of sober History.* They did heretofore in a manner engross the Monopoly of all the Wit and Fancy both of Greece and Rome: Insomuch, that 'tis hardly possible for a man well vers'd in the Greek and Latin Tongues, to be a stranger to the antient Geography of these Places: And Pliny, who was in nothing less erroneous, than in this part of his natural History of these Islands, does honour the Bay wherein they are situate, with the Title of Sinus claritatis literarum. A large Encomium, and such as no other aggregate body of Islands had equal right to. The Japan, Philippine, and Molucco Islands in the Oriental Ocean, are far beyond these for number; but the only thing they are sought for is some natural products peculiar to their Soil and Climate, in which commendation, they do not exceed

To the Reader.

ered the late discoveries in the American Ocean; but we find not that the World was ever beholding to the one, or the other, for the Propagation of Learning or Civility. Nor is it only famous for the early rise of Humane Learning and civil Culture, in the days of Gentilism; but also for the early appearance of the more glorious Sun-shine of the Heavenly Doctrin of the Gospel: St. John the Divine, honoured in the Oracles of God, with the peculiar Title of the Disciple whom Jesus loved, was once an Inhabitant of these Islands; where he founded the Christian Religion, and writ that Divine and Mysterious Book, which was indeed to him Apocalypse, but to all future ages Apocryphia. St. Paul, that great Apostle of the Gentiles, did often cross this Sea, to plant the Doctrin of Salvation in all the neighbouring Shores of Europe and Asia. And in future ages, when the Divine Providence raised up a Christian Emperour to protect his Church from persecution, these Islands were the very centre of once the most Orthodox and learned Church in the

To the Reader.

the World. To whom we owe not only the transmitting the Holy Scriptures to our knowledge, but also the digesting the Doctrin of them into Articles of Faith, the defense of Truth against all invasion of Errour, the faithful Records of most pure and primitive Tradition, the clear Exposition of many obscure passages, which without their direction, might have been at this day unintelligible, and the great advantage of many learned and elaborate Volumes of Orthodox Divinity, both Polemical and Practick. And of all those many different Sects of Christianity in the East, they have to this day most firmly retain'd the ancient Truths, and made the least Deviation into Errour. If that ignorance which those barbarous extinguishers of learning, the Turks, keep them in, renders that afflicted Nation obnoxious to be impos'd upon, and incapable of knowing better, it deserves rather our pity, than our contempt and scorn. It is rather a Miracle of Gods gracious Providence, that under such tyrannous Masters, and such proud and contemptuous enemies of

the

To the Reader.

the common name of Christianity, *the* light of Evangelical Truth *is* not only dim'd, but utterly extinct, *as* it has happ'ned in the Latin Church in Africa, once inferiour to none for purity of Doctrin, and piety and learning in their Professours. Yet this cannot be deny'd them; but that they accord with us in many things wherein we differ from the Romish Church. I may add this more, that in the Sacrament of the Eucharist, the Greek Church doth not bear that conformity or similitude with the Romish Church, as the great Champions for Popery would affix upon them. And that will easily appear in these particulars. 1. They use not the Elevation of the Host. 2. No carrying it in Procession. 3. The People stand when they receive it. 4. They give it in both kinds to all. 5. The bread is of a common sort before Consecration. It is besides, the business of this Preface, to enlarge upon the present State of the Greek Church, which the reverend Author hath in some measure done in his account of Samos, and Mount Athos: And that subject is more largely handl'd by a late learned

learned Author * in the Latin and
English *Tongues.* All that I shall add
is, that scarce any part of Greece has
less intermixture with the Turks than
these Isles, where the Greek Language and Religion is less intrench'd upon. There are no less than twenty
Bishops in the Archipelago, some with
the Title of Metropolite, as Metelyn and Methymia; others with the
Title of Arch-Bishop, as Samos, and
Andros, and some with the bare Title
of Bishop, as Sciathus. Yet neither
of the two first differ from the last in
any thing, but in Title, or priority of
Place. Their jurisdiction is alike, it
being ordinary here for a Metropolite,
and an Arch-Bishop to be without a
Suffragan. The reason is, because of
the great Revolutions, many of the old
Bishopricks are lost, and the ancient
frame of Ecclesiastical Polity much
alter'd. The Patriarch continues the
Title of Metropolite *upon all the places
that formerly were so,* and the Title
of Arch-Bishop, upon those that depend
immediately upon the Patriarch, without any subjection to a Metropolite,

* Smith's remarks upon the Turks.

al-

although they have no Bishop under their jurisdiction. The following Treatise giveth an account of three Islands of the Archipelago, and Mount Athos, the Great Academy for the Greek Clergy. In all these places, he liv'd, and writes nothing, but what he saw, or what he receiv'd from the constant Tradition of the places: So that as to matters of fact, he may be better rely'd upon than those that write of places to which they are great strangers. For the Truth of what is related, is the main Postulatum of an History.

A

A DESCRIPTION

Of the ISLE of

SAMOS

AND

Of its present State at this Day.

*Amos*, is one of the greatest, and most remarkable Islands of the *Archipelago*, situate near the Continent of *Asia*. It is well known that this was the Country of *Pythagoras*, and once was Govern'd by Kings of her own, and has made stout resistance against *Athens*, what time they both liv'd under a Democratical Government. The ruins which yet are to be seen

B there

there are a Testimony of her former greatness and wealth. But this Island hath been subject to great changes and revolutions, even to utter desertion of Inhabitants for many Years. Yet it being my main intent to give an account of its present State, I shall wave the former Transactions of Ancient times, whereof there is frequent mention amongst Historians, and proceed to a survey of its condition in these Modern Times, under the *Turkish* Empire; how it is now Govern'd; what Revenues it yields, with a Geographical Description of the Country.

It is certain, that what time it pleas'd God for our sins to permit the *Turks* to subdue *Constantinople*, and the *Archipelago*, the Island of *Samos* was totally dispeopl'd. Afterwards one *Kilitch Aly Basha* arrived here, and Landing with a small Company to Hunt, was so taken with the place, that he was resolv'd to ask leave of the Grand Signior, to re-people the Island: Which

Which having done, he transported several Families from all the Voisinage especially from *Metelyne*, so that by degrees, it became full of Inhabitants, and now counts to the number of 18 Towns and Villages, which I shall now describe according to their Situation.

The Isle of *Samos* is 26, or 27 *French* Leagues in compass, and lies in length East and West. At the West end it has the Isle of *Nicaria*, some twelve Miles distant: The East end is so near the Continent of *Asia*, that in some places men can Discourse one with another from the two Shores. This nearness of the East end of *Samos* to the Continent of *Asia*, causes a narrow Frith about six Miles in length, no where above 3 Miles in breadth, which by reason of little Islands in it, is a great Nest of Pirats, whom no Ships that come into this Strait can escape, but by putting to Shore on each side, where they are in equal danger of being made a Prey. These Pirats for the most part are either

either from *Malta*, *Legorn*, *Savoy*, or *Sardinia*.

At the entrance into this Streight, which the *Turks* call *Dardbogazy*, i.e. The Mouth of the Streight, lies all along the Mountain for the space of a Mile, the place where the Old City of *Samos* stood, remarkable yet for some remainders of the Walls and ruins of old Churches, and large Stones, some 3, some 4, some 5 yards long, besides many Marbles and Pillars, notwithstanding the many choice pieces carried away by the *Venetians*, when they were Lords of the *Archipelago*. But the *Greeks* at this day dare not touch a Stone, so much as to Build with, for fear of Imprisonment by the *Turks*, under colour of having found a Treasure in those old Ruins. And being once Imprison'd upon such a pretence, they are sure to lye fast till all they have be seiz'd.

These Ruins are no less than six miles in compass. Upon the same Mountain in the middle of a deep and large Grotto, stands a Church Dedi-

<small>Old Samos</small>

Dedicated to the Virgin *Mary*, known there by the name of Παναγία Σπιλιάνι, * *Panagia Spiliani*, or The moſt Holy Virgin of the Grotto. All the *Samians* pay great Devotion to this place, not only in honour of the Virgin *Mary*, but for the belief of many Miracles there done. Here is alſo an artificial Channel, ſix Miles long, drawn from a River of a perpetual ſtream, which beſides the Mills it drives, does water the Country in times of greateſt drought. This water ariſing near the Village of the *Arnhauts* (of whom we ſhall ſpeak more hereafter) becomes large enough by new ſupplies of other Currents, to deſerve the name of a River, and is that which the Ancients call'd *Imbraſus*.

   At the bottom of the aforeſaid Mountain, where Old *Samos* ſtood, towards *Scirus*, lye the Ruins of an old Haven for Galleys; the *Samians* call it *Tegani*, i. e. *Baſon*, from its roundneſs. Near to which Port ſtands a little Church Dedicated

* *Panagia Spiliani*, St. *Maries of the Cave Spiliani*, from Σπήλαιον

to * *St. Nicholas*, but now become a Refuge for the Mariners, who come privately to fetch Water from a Well hard by, that has a most excellent Spring: Yet here is always a strict Watch kept, one by Day, and two by Night, to carry Intelligence to the next *Aga*, or the next *Caddee*, what Ships come in, whence they are, and whither bound; And if the *Aga*, or *Caddee*, happen to hear of any Ships coming by some other Messenger, before he that is to Watch, brings the News, he is sure to receive 500 Bastinadoes upon the Soles of his Feet for his neglect.

* *St. Nicholas.*

Over-against the Old City, about a Mile distant to the West, stands the New, now known by the name of Μεγάλη χωρα, *Megale Chora*, or the great Town, because it is bigger than the rest of the Isle. Here the principal Men of the Isle have their residence, *i. e.* the Arch-bishop, the *Caddee*, with three or four *Turkish* Families, the *Aga*, with ten or a dozen other *Turks* to assist him

* *Megale Chora*, or *New Samos*.

him in the Execution of his Charge.

The *Caddees* Office is to pronounce Law, and the *Aga*'s to put it into Execution, and to Levy all Taxes whatsoever. There are many who submit themselves to the Jurisdiction of the Arch-bishop, especially the Ecclesiasticks. But if any Man rest unsatisfied with the Arch-bishops Judgment, he may appeal to the *Caddee*. There are very few *Turks* in this Isle, besides the forementioned. They had a Mosque, but the *Venetians* batter'd it down the first time they came with their Fleet to subdue the Island to their obedience, and to oblige them to contribution. But the *Samians* at first refus'd to pay Contribution, or to appear before the General, but made their escape into the Mountains, fearing the *Venetians* would soon be repuls'd by the *Turks*, and they be chastis'd for so quick a Revolt. But when the great Town was taken, and plunder'd, and the Mosque in it quite batter'd down, the *Aga* and *Caddee*, gave permission to the Islanders to pay a yearly tribute of 80000 Dollers or Crowns to the *Venetians*. Yet after the Peace made, when the *Turks* were re-establish'd, they would neither repair their batter'd Mosque, nor build a new one, for fear of some such casualty. Out of a Superstition they have, not to build a Mosque, but only where they are confident it shall never be profan'd by *Christian* violence.

Upon the coming of a new *Caddee*, or a new *Aga*, the Chief of the Villages assemble at the great Town, or upon any publick Affair which concerns the whole Island, especially upon the coming of the Officer appointed to gather the Poll-Money, called *Haratch*; Which is the only Revenue the Grand Signior receives out of this Island, all other the Revenues of the place, are all such as they call it, (a) *Vacouf*, that is Lands as we in *England* call Church Lands, especially Collegiate Churches, to which the Great Mosques in *Turkey* bear a great resemblance; for they have alwayes a Nursery of Men train'd up only to Sacred Employments; and a Governour, who is

(a) *Vacouf* amongst the *Turks*, are all such Lands as

called

called *Sheich*, and under him other principal Men, 'that are well maintain'd, and out of whose number a *Sheich* is chosen upon any vacancy. These Colleges they call *Medrasa*, and they are always close by the great Mosque,

to say, Consecrated to Religious use, and they belong wholly to the great Mosque at (a) *Tophana*, by *Galata*, over against the Grand Signiors *Seraglio* at *Constantinople*.

(a) *Tophana*, is the House of Guns, and it has its name from the use it is put to, being the great Store-house for the Grand Signior's Ordnance, and Artillery, and the place of Residence for the *Topgy-Basha*, or Master of the Ordnance to the Grand Signior.

In other parts of the Empire, all Males that are not *Turks*, from 14 years and upwards, do pay yearly three Dollers a Head, but in *Samos* only Married Men are oblig'd. Yet if a Married Man dies leaving a Male Child, the *Haratch* shall be demanded for the Child, though he be but a sucking Infant. Strangers that come, pay this *Haratch*, Married or un-married. In like manner, the *Samians* that quit their Country to exercise any Trade or Traffick elsewhere in the Empire, do pay this *Haratch*, though un-married. When the

the Collector of this Poll-Money (whom they call *Haratchgy*) comes, he first goes to the *Caddee*, and shews him the Imperial Mandat. Whereupon the *Caddee* summons the chief Men of every Village, whom they call *Proesti*, to come before him at the great Town, where having read to them the Imperial Mandat, he charges them to take all possible care for the speedy Levying of the Tribute, which they promising, are dismiss'd. Then the *Haratchgy* goes to every Village, demanding of the *Papas*, or the Minister of the place an exact Catalogue of the names of those that are oblig'd to pay, which if the *Papas* fail to do, or omit any names that should have been put in, he is sure to be laid down, and drub'd. There is no excuse for any person, and he that cannot pay, is clapt into Chains, and led about as a Prisoner, till he has either sold his Goods, or beg'd Money to defray the charge of this Poll-Money.

The *Caddee* is sent hither by one
of

the Isle of SAMOS.

of the *Caddileskers*, whereof there are two, the one for *Europe*, call'd the *Romily Caddilesker*, the other for *Asia*, called the *Anodal Caddilesker*. These two are next to the *Mufty* for Dignity and Power, and take place next to him. By one of these are all the *Caddees* sent to their respective charges. The Perquisits of the *Caddee* of *Samos* arise from the Courts of Judicature, where he is President: And upon the Death of any Person, he takes an Inventory of all his Goods, which being priz'd, he takes three *per Cent*, according to their value. But he meddles not with the Lands, being all appropriated to the aforesaid Mosque of *Tophana*: But if any Man dye without Issue Male, the *Aga* has power to seise his Lands, and to sell them to whom he pleases. Neither Male nor Female can inherit the Lands of their Mother, but they fall to the *Aga*, who has power to sell or dispose of them as he thinks fit. If a Man leave his Lands uncultivated for seven Years,

the

the *Aga* has power to sell them, and to demand satisfaction for those dues, that might have accru'd to him, if the Lands had been cultivated, those seven Years. We will return to the remaining part of the Description of *Megale Chore*, and other remarkable places of the Isle.

The whole Town, and all the Gardens about it, are supply'd with Water from two (*a*) Fountains, that of the two, whose Water is sweeter to the tast, is called *Platanos*, the other *Messaki*. There are but six Churches, and those small ones. Nor is it expedient in that Country, that any thing which concerns the Christian Religion should make any outward appearance of Magnificence, or costliness, least it should provoke the envy aud avarice of their proud Masters to Sacrilegious rapine. On the South side of the City lyes a large plain, by a word mixt with *Greek* and *Latin*, call'd (*b*) *Megalocampos*, being the greatest Plain in the Isle; which by reason of abundance of standing Water

(a) *Plin. l. 5. c. 31. Fontes Eucarto, Leucothea.*

(b) *Megalocampos.*

Water wherewith it perpetually stagnates, yields no benefit, but great nuisance to the neighbouring Inhabitants: Yet is it like to continue still a Fenny Marsh, so long as the Tyrannous Government of the Country gives so small Encouragement to the improvement of Lands. The Mariners that sail by that Coast are the better for't, to whom it affords fresh Water enough to furnish a whole Fleet, in four streams that issuing from this Fen, disembogue themselves into the Sea, some six Miles distant from the Fen: Yet the Coast is so open, that no Vessel can ride there but when the Wind is in the North.

Beyond this plain a large space of fruitful Lands, water'd with the foremention'd *Imbrasus*, belongs to a Monastry in *Patmos*, giv'n by a *Greek* Architect, one of the first Planters, who dying without Issue, left all he had to the said Monastry. Beyond these Lands which belong to the Monastry of *Patmos*, upon the same River stands a village of some 200

Imbrasus.

200 Houses, with one Church; It's called (a) *Mily*, or the Mills, from that abundance of Water Mills, which *Imbrasus* drives there. Here Lemmons and Oranges are so plentiful, that 500 may be bought for one Doller. Westward of this Village lies (b) *Pagontas*, Situate on a Hill bedeck'd with Trees, the most healthful and pleasant Village of the Island. It hath no less than 300 Houses, and two Churches, and is enrich'd by the Manufacture of Silks. Some three Miles distant from this Town, towards the Mountain, lies (c) *Spatharei*, a small Village consisting of about 50 Houses, and one Church, but famous for making Pitch, which they sell at *Megale Chore* for three quarters of a Doller, and sometimes a Doller the *Kintal*. (d) Their way of making is like *Pliny*'s description of it, *l.*16.*c.*11.

(a) *Mily*.

(b) *Pagontas.*

(c) *Spatharei.*

(d) Their way of making Pitch is thus. They take *Sapines*, that is to say, that part of Firs, or other unctuous Trees as is betwixt the Root and the Boughs, so far as it hath no Knots; and shaving away the extreme parts, they leave only that which is nearest to the middle, and the Pith: That which remains they call *Dadi*, (from the old *Greek* word Δαδις, whence comes the Latin *Tæda*) These *Dadi*, or Torches, they cleave into small pieces, and laying them on a Furnace,

nace, put fire to the upper part, till they are all burnt, the Liquor in the mean time running from the Wood, and let out from the bottom of the Furnace into a hole made in the Ground, where it continues like Oyl; Then they put Fire to't, and stir it about till it thicken, and has a consistence; Then putting out the Fire, they cast Chalk upon it, and draw it out with a Vessel, and lay it in little places cut out of the Ground, where it receives both its form, and a firmer consistence for easie Transportation.

Over-against the Village of *Spatharei*, about a quarter of a Mile distant from Shore lies a little Island a Mile in compass, called (a) *Samio Paulo*, or Little *Samos*; furnish'd with a safe Harbour against all Winds towards great *Samos*. This Island abounds with a peculiar sort of Flower, which from a Fragrance it hath, like unto *Musk*, the People call (b) *Muskoulia*, others call them *Coree*. This Flower has that esteem in *Turky*, that they are sent for as far as to *Constantinople*, whither they are transplanted with much care into their choicest Gardens. The Grand Signior wears it ordinarily in his Turbant, and by his Example, makes it a Fashionable wear among the Grandees of his Court. It hath this

(a) *Samio Paulo*, or little *Samos*, formerly *Narthecus*.

(b) *Mouskoulia*.

this quality, that time doth not decay, but augment the Fragrance of its Smell.

Three Miles diftant from *Spatharei*, on the Hill fide, ftands the Village of (a) *Pyrgos*, confifting of about an 100 Houfes, and 2 Churches: Here is the Choiceft Honey. Above this Village ftands a fmall Village and Colony of the (b) *Arnaouts*, or *Albanians*; for fo is that Nation at this day called by the *Greeks* and *Turks*: And they have many Colonies in the Empire, being encourag'd with fpecial priviledges and immunities from the Grand Signior: yet they lofe not their Language (which in all likelihood is the old *Illyrian*) for it is not underftood by any of their Neighbour Nations; nor is it an Of-fpring of the *Slavonick*. Their Religion is the fame with the *Greek*.

Six Miles from *Pyrgos*, towards the South, lies (d) *Platanos*, fo call'd, from abundance of Plain Trees there formerly. This Town hath

(a) *Pyrgos*.

(b) *Arnaouts* Village.

(c) *Platanos*.

the Isle of SAMOS.

hath at least 300 Houses, and two Churches, and is remarkable for its good Air. Both the Men and Women being generally longer Liv'd here, than any where else in the Island. Their Waters hereabouts abound with Champinions, a great relief to the Poor, when the word is given out for publick permission to Fish. Which word with them is *Anoixe to libarintous*.

Six Miles from hence, towards the West, lies a Village of some 200 Houses, and two Churches, call'd (a) *Maratha-campos*, from the abundance of (b) Fennel thereabouts, which the *Greeks* call *Maratha*. This Village looks toward *Patmos*, from whence it is distant some Forty Miles.

(a) *Maratha-campos.*
(b) *Gal. Fenouil.* Μάραθρον

Three Miles from this Village lies a small Hermitage, by the Name of (c) St. *George*'s Hermitage, where two or three Hermits of *Patmos*, commonly reside. Not far from this Hermitage is a Grotto upon the top of a Mountain of most difficult access, which the People, by Tradition

(c) Saint *George*'s Hermitage.

dition do believe was *Pythagoras*'s retiring place; it hath now a little Church, call'd Παναγία Φανερομένη, Or the Blessed Virgin appearing; Because of a Tradition that the Blessed Virgin *Mary* has here appeared, and done Miracles. The Bones of Dead Men that lie scatter'd hereabouts, give occasion to believe, that those that remained when the Island was deserted, made their escape hither; it being a Retreat of most difficult access: And the inner Parts of this Mountain are not well discover'd, in asmuch as people are seen to appear, and observ'd to gather Chesnuts, none of the Inhabitants of the Valley knowing any thing more of them.

This (*a*) Mountain is called *Kerkis*, the highest of the whole Island, from whose top may be seen the greatest part of the Isles of the *Archipelago*: It is cover'd with Snow almost all the Year, and hath a Lake on the very top, well stor'd with Eels. Here is a Chappel Consecrated to the Prophet *Elias*

(a) *Mons. Cercetius.* Plin. *l.* 5. *c.* 31.

(*a*) *Elias*, whither many resort for Devotion: Here is likewise a Grotto, with another Chappel; which hath no Tradition of its Name or Dedication; yet many go thither to say their Prayers, and at *Easter* time it is much frequented. This chappel, and Grotto stand directly over against the Isle of *Nicaria*, some 12 Miles from hence.

(*a*) Elias's Chappel.

That which increaseth the Religious esteem of this latter Chappel, is, a Tradition, That Light has often appear'd in the Night time, which the People conceive to be a Warning of some Holy Reliques that lyes here yet undiscover'd, and so neglected.

Upon the same Mountain, some six Miles distant, towards the North, stands another Hermitage; besides which, in a spacious Grotto, stands a little Church, Dedicated to the Virgin *Mary*. It hath but one way of access, and that up a steep Precipice so extremely dangerous, that it is called (*b*) Παναγία εις τὸ κακοπέρχτον, or St. *Maries*, upon the bad passage.

(*b*) *Panagia eis to Cacoperaton.*

Five

Five Miles from *Maratha-campos*, towards the North, is the Village of (*a*) *Caſtanees*, ſo call'd, from abundance of Cheſnut-Trees about it. It has about 50 Houſes, and one Church. Not far from hence is the Hermitage of the Holy Trinity, where always two or three Hermits of the Monaſtry of *Patmos* do reſide.

(a) *Caſtany*

Two Miles from *Caſtany*, ſtands (*b*) *Leca*, a Village of 50 Houſes, and one Church.

(b) *Leca*.

Not far from *Leca* is the Monaſtry of (*c*) St. *George*, an Hoſpital for the (*d*) Monks of Mount *Sina*; it hath always four or five Prieſts, who look after the Revenues of the Hoſpital, which conſiſts chiefly in Wine.

(c) *Saint George's Monaſtry.*
(d) *Monks of Mount Sina.*

Higher upon the Hill-ſide, over againſt *Leca*, is a Covent of Monks of *Elias*; Men abſtracted from all ſecular employment, and they entertain all Paſſengers with what they have upon free coſt.

Six Miles from hence, towards *Megalocampos*, lyes (*e*) *Carlovaſy*, the

(d) *Carlovaſy.*

the greatest Town of this Island, next to *Megale Chore*. It is situate by the Sea-side, over against *Sio*, and the Castle of *Siatsky*, upon the Continent of *Asia*. It hath no less than 500 Houses, and 5 Churches. The Inhabitants are the Richest of any in the Isle, by reason of their Traffick by Sea to *Sio*, *Smyrna*, *Chios*, and other places. Their principal Merchandise are Onions, and Muscat Wine. Yet their Port is so expos'd to the North Wind, and unsafe a Road for any Vessels, that they are forc'd to load their Vessels a Shore, and so to thrust them off: And at their return, without any delay they draw up their Vessels to Land.

Three Miles Eastward, from *Carlovasi* is the Town of (a) *Furni*, remarkable for those Earthen Jars, and Pitchers, and other Vessels, which formerly were so much in esteem by the *Greeks*, and *Romans*, and were peculiarly call'd *Samian* Vessels. The Town hath at least 200 Houses, and two Churches,

(a) *Furni.*

and has its name from the Furnaces where these Vessels are made. Besides this Town is a Fountain, whose stream is sufficient to make a Mill go; at the Spring-head is a Church, Consecrated to the Blessed Virgin, to which the Inhabitants of the Town pay great Devotion. From hence begins a row of Mountains, cover'd with Woods for the space of twenty Miles. It is furnish'd with all manner of Wood, fit for Architecture, as well for Vessels at Sea, as for Houses at Land, a great encrease to the *Aga's* Revenue; But the Chesnuts wherewith it abounds, are free for all Comers.

Upon the top of this Mountain is a Village call'd (a) *Vourlioté*, a Colony of *Vourla*, a small Town by *Smyrna*. It hath about an 100 Houses, and one Church. The greatest Employment of the Inhabitants, is to cut Wood, and make Pitch.

Within half a Mile of this Town is a Monastry of a douzen *Caloirs*, by the name of (b) *Panagia Touphronta*.

(a) *Vourlioté*.

(b) *Panagia Touphronta*.

The

the Iſle of SAMOS.

The Graſs about this Monaſtry in the Spring time is Venomous to all ſtrange Cattle; ſo that if an Horſe brought from a ſtrange place be put into the Grounds, in a ſhort time he ſhall ſwell and burſt: But the Horſes bred up about the Monaſtry, and the next Village, find no ſuch inconvenience at all.

Ten Miles from this Monaſtry Eaſtward, ſtands (a) *Vathy*, a Village of 400 Houſes, and four Churches, enriched with a Port, affording a ſafe Habour in all Winds but the South. But four Miles toward the North Eaſt lies another ſo well ſheltred with three little Iſlands, (call'd τȣ̃ πηλȣ̃ ͅησια, or the Iſles of Dirt,) that Veſſels may ride ſafely in all Winds. Theſe Iſlands are 20 Miles from *Scala nova*, a remarkable Port, and much frequented upon the Continent of *Aſia*. The great Traffick of this Town is in Wine, eſpecially Muſcat, which will hold good a whole Year, whereas that of *Carlovaſy* turns ſower after ſix months age. It is

(a) *Vathy*.

like-

likewise remarkable for Fishing.

(a) *Palaio-Castro.* Near to this stands (*a*) *Palaio-Castro*, or the *Old Castle* ; a Village of an 100 Houses and one Church. Here also are good Wines, especially Muscat.

(b) *Vourcaria.* Four Miles from hence is the Port (*b*) *Vourcaria*, near to which is a convenient place for making Salt. But the Inhabitants fearing a great Imposition from the *Turks*, will not be at the pains to make any, being content with what is brought them from *Mylos*, and *Naxos*, from which two Islands all the *Archipelago* is supply'd.

(c) ὁ Πισος κάμπος. Two Miles from hence lies a great Plain, call'd (*c*) ὁ Γισος κάμπος, *Ho pisos campos*, wherein rises a Fountain, whose only stream causes two Mills to go. This Plain is fruitful in Wheat, in Cotton, and the Grain of *Turky*, which the *Greeks* call Ἐρύσιμον, the *Latins Trio,* and the *French* peculiarly *Le bled de Turquie*, or the *Grain of Turky.* Here is a Church Dedicated to St. *John* the Divine; the Church is

the Isle of SAMOS.

is called (a) τῦ Θεολόγȣ. The Inhabitants have an opinion of Miracles here done, and have a Tradition, that St. *John*, as well as (b) St. *Paul* has been in *Samos*, which causes great resort to this place for Devotion.

(a) Ἐκκλησία Ἰωάννȣ τȣ̃ Θεολόγȣ.

(b) *Acts* 20. 15. Τῇ δὲ ἑτέρᾳ παρεβάλομεν εἰς Σάμον.

Four Miles hence, towards the North, stands *Mytelene*, a Village of some 200 Houses, and 2 Churches. It is a Colony of the Island *Mytelene*. This Village is but a Mile from *Megale Chore*, the principal place of the Island wherewith we begun, and so we have finish'd the Circuit of the whole Island, and the Geographical Description of the Villages in it. It remains, that we speak of some Monastrys yet untouch'd.

The Monastrys hitherto omitted, are but two, Σταυρὸς and Παναγία σὰ πέντε σπίτια.

1. Two Miles from the great Village is *Stauros*, or the Monastry of the *Cross*, wherein are 30 *Caloirs*. It is well endow'd with Lands, and a Farm House for Lay Fryers,

Fryers to Till their Ground. Besides it hath another Monastry depending upon it, where the Fryers chief Employment is to make Cloth, to do all other necessary work for the Service and Maintenance of the great Covent.

2. (*a*) *Panagia sta Pente Spitia*, which in Vulgar Greek signifies the *Blessed Virgin of the five Houses*. This maintains 60 *Caloirs*, and has a smaller Monastry at *Pagondas*, subservient to it, in like manner as the former. This Monastry is not subject to the Arch-Bishop, but only to the Patriarch of *Constantinople*.

The Island is well stor'd with Sheep and Goats; But every Sheep is redeem'd with two Aspers, and every Goat with one, payable to the *Vacouf* or great Mosque at *Tophana* in *Galata*. Yet were this Law literally put in execution, it were well for the People; but the *Agas* take the boldness to levy more, as they think fit. Nor can the People help themselves, the charge of Appeal being greater than the Pay-

(*a*) Spete, and Spition, *in vulgar Greek signifies an house, from* Hospitium. *The first corruption of that Tongue came from the mixture of Latin words.*

the Isle of SAMOS.

Payment injuriously exacted. And such is the Corruption of the *Turkish* Court, that the event of an Appeal would be as uncertain as the attempt unsafe.

Besides the *Aga* demands as his due, all the Butter he finds among the Inhabitants, what day soever he pitches upon to number their Flocks, in order to the gathering this *Vacouf* Money; which grievance arose by the inconsiderate bounty of a rich *Samian*, who to ingratiate with the *Aga*, presented him with a great quantity of Butter, since which time, the *Aga* has ever claim'd it as his due from all others.

The *Aga* is likewise presented by every man of stock with a Lamb and a Kid; which by a Charter obtain'd from the Grand Signior, the *Samians* have power to redeem with two Aspers and an half by the head, but the *Aga* exacts no less than five or six.

And now it is no wonder if this oppression by the *Turkish* Officers keep

keep the Inhabitants poor, ignorant, and low spirited. *Kilitch-Aly-Basha*, at his first coming to re-people the Island, brought none with him but men of low Fortunes, and the Tyranny they live under doth still keep them so. And the Malice of many slothful, but servile people among them, doth render it impossible for any person well affected to the Publick good, to effect any thing toward their Liberty, or redress of Grievances. For there wants not among the *Greeks* perpetual spies, that for their private ends, bring intelligence to the *Aga*'s Ministers of any motion made, or any word freely spoken towards the redress of Grievances. The *Aga*'s principal Engins are either those of his Family, (call'd *Musifarides*) or such creatures as lie dispers'd throughout the Island. Those of his Family, are his Secretaries and Interpreters: The latter sort are alwayes *Greeks*; for a *Turk* counts it a great dishonour to learn any *Christian* Language.

His Creatures abroad are the
Proesti,

(*a*) *Proesti*, or Chief of the Villages, whom he alwayes makes his Creatures, and they for private ends are very forward to acquaint him any thing that may please him. They are more zealous and forward to pay their Homage to a Turkish *Aga*'s House, than to serve Almighty God in his publick Worship; and as if Interest and Gain were their Godliness, they are more punctually careful to devote their time to a servile attendance in the outmost Gate of the *Aga*, among his Porters and meaner Servants, than in the solemn assembly of their fellow *Christians* in the Church of God. In so much, that though they are *Christians* by profession, yet on the most solemn days of publick Devotion, their greatest Religion is to wait at the *Aga*'s House, to bid him good morrow, when he goes out to attend his pleasure, to drink Coffee, and smoak Tobacco among his Servants, and to speak nothing but what may flatter his Pride, or serve his Avarice. There is no

(a) Πρεστις

Village

Village in the Island so small, that wants such pestilent Spirits as these.

Samos is not inferiour to any Island of the *Archipelago* for good Soil. They are not beholden to other Countrys for any thing but Iron and Salt; and this latter they might have, did not the oppression of the *Turks* discourage their Industry. They are well stor'd with Trees of all sorts, with Pitch, Cottons, Corn, Oyl, Honey, and Wine, of whose Lees they make abundance of *Aqua vitæ* in the Month of *October*, by them call'd *Asynchoretos*, ἀσυγχώρητος: For when they make their *Aqua vitæ*, all Passengers are invited to tast of it, which he that refuses, is branded with the name of Ἀσυγχώρητος, in these words, Ἐὰν θὲν ἤρθες να ἔσαι ἀσυγχώρητος; *If you will take none, you shall never obtain pardon.*

*Ἀσυγχώρητ*Ꙩ*, unforgiven.*

All the People of the Country are Labourers, excepting the *Musafarides*, who farm out their Lands, and make it their business to attend the

the *Aga*. Every Master of a Family is oblig'd to attend the *Aga* at such time as he puts all his Corn in a readiness to be measur'd. And then is one of the *Musafarides* sent, who is to be entertain'd at the charge of the Master of the Family, but instead of taking a Tenth of the Corn, which is strictly his due; he takes Money according to his own valuation of the price of Corn.

All Wines, *Aqua vitæ*, and Oyl, are Tith'd according to an ancient rate set down in the Court Rolls.

Heretofore there was no Imposition taken upon Silks, because it was a Manufacture exercis'd only by the hands of Women, 'till a certain *Aga* came, that desir'd a little to make him a Girdle; and being presented with a good handsome Basket full: The next year he demanded the like quantity every where as his due.

The Habit of the *Samians* is like the *Turks*: A long Vest, like our Cassock, down to the Heels with a Girdle about the Loins, and over

it

it a loose Garment, like a Batchelour of Arts Gown. The Women likewise imitate the *Turkish* Women in their Apparel, girded about the Loins, a white Vail over their Heads. The young Women let their hair hang down behind, in a long Lock plaited, and ty'd at the end with a Silver or Guilt Chain.

In former times, the greatest part of the Isles of the *Archipelago* were under the Jurisdiction of the Arch-Bishop of *Rhodes*; and this Isle had a Bishop that was Suffragan to that Arch-Bishop. But since the last re-peopling of the Isle, it has been under the Patriarch of *Constantinople*, who bestow'd it upon the great Church of *Constantinople*, and sent a Vicar to collect all the Ecclesiastical Revenues. And in this condition it continu'd for an hundred years, 'till the People of the Isle did petition the Patriarch to let them have an Arch-Bishop, which accordingly he did, and appointed them the Bishop of *Nicaria* for their Suffragan; but that Island being too poor

poor to maintain a Bishop at this day the Arch-Bishop of *Samos* has now no Suffragan at all.

When a new Arch-Bishop comes, he shews his Patent from the Grand Signior to the *Caddee*; then summons all the *Proesti* of the Villages, to whom having read his Patent, he has it Register'd in the publick Records of the Island. This done, they all accompany him to the Cathedral Church, where after the Reading of his Institutions, given by the Patriarch, he is plac'd in the Archiepiscopal Throne, where every one comes to kiss his Hand, and he bestows upon them his Benediction; and then makes them a Speech (if he find himself of sufficient capacity to do't.) This is the way of his Investiture into the Arch-Bishoprick of *Samos* and *Nicaria*.

At his first coming, the *Papas*, or Parish Priest of the Church of his Residence presents him 15, or 20 Dollers; they of the other Churches according to their Abilities.

The first year of his coming, every Parish Priest pays him 4 Dollers, and the following years 2. Every Lay-man pays him 48 Aspers, and the following years 24. The rest of his Revenues comes in by Ordinations and Marriages. One part of the Island come to *Megale Chore*, where he Resides, for Licenses to Marry, the other part to his Vicar General at *Carlovasi*. The *Samians* pay one Doller for a License; all Strangers two: But he that comes after first Marriage for a License for a second, or third, pays three or four. Since *Samos* has been an Arch-Bishoprick, there has been hitherto but eight; 1. *Athanasius*; 2. *Anthimus*; 3. *Parthenius*; 4. *Cornelius*; 5. *Christophorus*; 6. *Neophytus*; 7. *Joseph* (who writ this History in vulgar *Greek*) and *Philaretus* that now succeeds him. Of whom here is a short account.

Athanasius, a Native of the Isle, and a Marry'd Priest, but his Wife dying about the time of his promotion, took upon him the Habit

bit of a *Caloir*, he was Arch-Bishop 20 years,

Anthimus, surnam'd *Judas*, because at the Ceremony of the Patriarch's washing the Feet of twelve Priests on *Maunday Thursday*, he being one, had the name of *Judas*. The Patriarch of *Constantinople*, in imitation of our Saviour, doth every year, on *Maunday Thursday*, Wash the Feet of twelve Men in Holy Orders, who are at that time called the twelve Apostles; and every Priest hath at that time the name of some particular Apostle. After he had been Arch-Bishop 15 years, upon a Complaint made against him by the Islanders to the *Capitan Basha*, or Admiral of the *Turkish* Fleet, he was clapt into prison, whence being releas'd by a sum of Money, he became afterwards Arch-Bishop of *Cæsarea* in *Cappadocia*.

Parthenius a *Theban*, was Translated from the Arch-Bishoprick of *Patras* to *Samos*, where he presided 12 years, only under the Title of προεδρως, or President; but after he he had passed 12 years under this meaner and unusual Title, he was admitted to the full Rights and Dignity of an Arch-Bishop.

Cornelius of *Metelyne* was deposed by the Patriarch of *Constantinople*, after he had sat six years.

Christophorus a *Samian*, was clapt into the Galleys by the *Venetian* Admiral, for not paying Contribution to the *Venetians*, at the appointed time; for hapning to be Arch-Bishop in the beginning of that War between the *Turks* and *Venetians* (so calamitous to all the *Greek* Isles) the *Venetians* then Masters at Sea, forc'd all the *Archipelago* to contribution. He to secure his poor flock, the *Samians*, from immediate Plunder, Rapine, Captivity, and other Insolencies, did engage for raising the demanded Contribution, which was an high sum for that place, but was not able to make good his promise within the appointed time; because of the Peoples poverty: Whereupon the *Venetian* Admiral, without any respect

respect to his Religion as a *Christian*, or to his place and quality as an Arch-Bishop, did most Barbarously put him into the Gallies, a punishment commonly imposed upon *Turkish* Captives, or such *Christians* only as were gross and notorious Malefactours, and judicially condemn'd for capital Crimes.

Neophytus of *Siphanto* sat 6 years, and deceased in the Island.

After him came *Joseph Georgirene*, of the Island of *Milos*, who was Consecrated, *October* 7. 1666. He sat here five years, till after the taking of *Candie*, the *Turks* grew more populous, and consequently more abusive: So that wearied with their injuries, he retired to the Holy *Grotto* of the *Apocalypse*, in the Isle of *Patmos*.

After he had voluntarily retir'd from his Arch-Bishoprick, the Patriarch of *Constantinople* did presently substitute in his place *Philaretus* of the Isle of *Siphanto*.

And thus much concerning the Arch-Bishop of *Samos*, his Investiture

stiture, his Jurisdiction, and his Revenue. Proceed we to the Clergy, that under him have the Cure of Souls. And these not only in *Samos*, but throughout the whole extent of the whole *Greek* Church, are always dignifi'd and distinguish'd by the peculiar title of Γαπᾶς, *Papas* which signifies a Father, because in spiritual matters within the bounds of their Cure, they are Fathers, as well to Feed as to Govern.

(a) *Of those whom the Greeks call* Papas, *or Parochial Priests.*

The *Papas* in the bounds of his Parish is oblig'd to perform all those sacred Offices which the *Greek* Ritual requires. They are not only allow'd to Marry, but oblig'd to do't, before they enter into the Order of Priest-hood. And not only those *Greek* Priests that live under the Patriarch of *Constantinople*, but also those *Greeks* that in *Sicily*, *Calabria*, and in the Islands under the State of *Venice* do embrace the *Romish* Religion, are by allowance of the Pope permitted to Marry. And such Men (though Marry'd)

the Isle of SAMOS.

Marry'd) are commonly Ordained Priests at *Rome* it self, by some *Greek* Bishop of the *Romish* Religion in the College of *Greeks* at *Rome*, and in that of *Spain*, and in that called *Madonna del Populo*: Yet the *Greek* Church, for that esteem they have of a Monastick Life, do never advance a Parish Priest to a Bishoprick, except his Wife be Dead, or Divorc'd from him, and he take upon him the Habit and Profession of a *Caloir*.

A Marry'd Man, that would take Orders, is required to declare, that he has been but once Marry'd, and that his Wife was neither a Widow, nor a Slave, nor the Daughter of a Slave, or under the reproach of an Harlot: This done, he comes to a Confessour, who among other Sins, doth particularly put him upon the Confession of those Sins that by the Canon would exclude him from entring into Orders. And though his Confessour give him a good Testimony, yet a Week before the Ordination, the Bishop doth

doth openly in the Church charge all the Assembly under the Peril of Excommunication, if they know him guilty of any Crime that may render him unworthy of Holy Orders, to reveal it before the next Sunday: Which if any Man do, and make good his Accusation, he is denied Holy Orders; if the Accuser be found to Impeach him falsely, he is Excommunicated for his false Accusation, and the other Ordain'd. After the *Candidate* for Holy Orders has thus made his way, the day before he enters into Priests Orders, he comes to the Metropolite, who having try'd whether he Read and Write without false Pronuntiation, or mis-spelling; and being satisfied in that point, doth presently Ordain him Sub-deacon and Deacon, and the next day Priest, if he be of sufficient Age. The Age for a Reader is 18; For a Sub-Deacon, 20; For a Deacon, 25. For a Priest, 30; Nevertheless it is left to the Discretion of the Metropolite, to dispense with the Canon,

as

as he shall see occasion, according to the example of *Anicetus*, who Ordained St. *Eleutherius* a Priest at 18, and Bishop of *Illyrium* at 20. If a *Papas* Marry a second time, he is deprived of his Orders, and called ever after *Apopapas*. But nothing hinders the Widow of a Priest to Marry again.

The *Papas* is obliged to Read Prayers, and Administer the Sacrament every Sunday and Holyday. The day before a Sacrament, he is to sing the Vespers, and after Supper, to rehearse a Prayer call'd the Ἀπόδειπνον; if after that Prayer said, he chance to Eat or Drink that Night, he is oblig'd to go to Church, and say that Prayer again: Likewise that Night he is not allow'd to lye with his Wife.

Every Parishioner is obliged to bring to Church a Loaf to the Weight of seven or eight pounds, which is mark'd with these three words; Ἰησῦς Χριςὸς νικᾶ : *Jesus Christ overcomes*. Of this Bread the Priest distributes to every one a

Mor-

Morsel, and the rest goes to himself.

If any man desire the Sacrament upon other days than Sundays or Holidays, he sends to the Priest the day before, to prepare himself according to the Canon. The next Morning the Priest sends to him to bring with him what is necessary for Celebration, *viz.* a Loaf, marked as before, a Wax Taper of two Aspers, and Incense of one Asper, (for they never Celebrate without a lighted Taper, and Incense) and a Quart of Wine, and three Aspers in Money: What is left of the Bread and Wine, goes to the Priest with three Aspers. He that leaves it to the Priest to provide necessaries, brings with him 15 Aspers.

The Parish Priests, excepting those that are very ancient, or Widowers, never confess any. That employment is left ordinarily to the *Caloirs* of the Order of St. *Basil*, whereof there wants not some every where dispersed throughout the

the whole *Greek* Church, to beg Almes for the Monks of *Athos*, from whence they are sent. Yet neither they, nor any Parish Priest confess any without a particular Licence from the Metropolite, who doth enjoyn them under a Mortal Sin, not to exact any Money for Absolution. But if after Absolution, the Penitent offer any thing, they receive it. If the Penitent desires any Prayers to be said for him in some Monastry of Mount *Athos*, he gives Money in consideration of the Prayers to be said for him.

If the Parish Priest have any Lands, he thinks it no shame to Till them himself. But he resides constantly in the Parish, to be ready upon all occasions for the Sick, to whom he says the Prayers appointed by the Church for Sick people.

If a Woman be in Child-birth, he is sent for to say some Prayers appointed for that occasion; nor can the company that come to assist the Woman in her Travail leave the House, 'till the Priest come and
perform

perform the Sacred Ceremonies appointed by the Church, for Women in Child-bed; accounting it a great contempt of God, and a thing ominous and of ill foreboding to the succefs of the perfon in Labour, to neglect their folemn addrefs to God in the prayers appointed by publick Authority for that Emergency.

(a) *Of their Women in Child-bed.*

A Woman (*a*) after Child-birth ftirs not abroad, neither to Church, nor to other Houfes, till 40 days be expir'd. Then fhe is brought to the Church Door, where the Prieft having faid the Prayers appointed for that occafion, fhe is permitted to go to Church, or to other Houfes.

(b) *Pædobaptifm.*

The Children ordinarily are not (*b*) Baptiz'd till 40 days after Birth, fometimes, under pretence of the Parents or Goffips abfence, not till half a Year, a whole Year, or more. But this is alwayes in cafe the Child be healthy and ftrong; for upon the leaft fufpition of the Childs being weak, or likely to dye, the
Prieft

Priest is sent for by the Parents, and without any further Ceremony, the Child is Baptized in this manner.

N. N. **The servant of God doth Baptize thee, in the Name of the Father,** Amen. **Of the Son,** Amen. **And of the Holy Ghost, from henceforth and for evermore,** Amen.

In private Baptism they use only Water, Oyl, and a Lamp burning before the Picture of the Virgin *Mary.* For there is no House so poor, which has not the Picture of the Blessed Virgin, or some other Saint, before which they pray, Morning and Night, after they have lighted a Lamp.

In publick Baptism, the Child is brought to the Church Porch, where after the Priest has said an Exorcism, the Child is brought to the Font, and being interrogated by the Priest, the God-father makes answer, and rehearseth the Creed thrice. Then the Priest Consecrates the Water, which being hot he he pours into't Oil Olive, and Anoints the Child on several parts of the Body. The Child is Anointed on the Forehead, Mouth, Ears, Breast, Hands, Knees, and Feet with these words at every place; *The Seal of the Gift of the Holy Spirit.* Then the God-father claps a Cross to the Childs Breast: This done, the Priest takes the Child stark naked, and bath's him all over thrice in the Water, saying the same words as you had in private Baptism. After the third Bathing, he pours some of the Water upon the Child's Head: Then delivering the Child into the hands of the God-Fathers, he puts a Shirt on the Child, with these words; *Jesus Christ our merciful God, cloathed with Light, give thee a bright Garment.*

Marriage. All the *Greeks* of the Island that (*b*) Marry, first obtain a License of the Arch-Bishop, or his Grand Vicar: Then the Priest having examined if they have any Legal prohibition of affinity, or otherwise; either at the Church, or their own Houses;

Houses, Marrys them in this manner. After the Reading of that part of the Liturgy which concerns Marriage, and the parties enterchanging a Ring, the Priest takes two Garlands made like Crowns, and signing them with the sign of the Cross, he puts one on the Bridegrooms Head, with these words:

The Servant of God N. N. is Crown'd to the Servant of God A. A. in the name of the Father, the Son, and the Holy Ghost, henceforth and for ever.

The like is done to the Bride, and then the Epistle and Gospel appointed for the Occasion is Read. Then he that gives them in Marriage, first Kisses the Garlands, and all the Company, in Testimony of their wishing Joy to the Married Parties.

On *Maunday Thursday*, which is an high day with the *Greeks*,* they Consecrate Bread, and pour upon it consecrated Wine, with these words:

* *Sacrament for the Sick.*

The

𝕬 𝔇𝔢𝔰𝔠𝔯𝔦𝔭𝔱𝔦𝔬𝔫 𝔬𝔣

The Union and Conformation of the Holy Body, and Precious Blood, Amen.

This Bread is laid up till the firſt Sunday after *Eaſter*, and then the Prieſt in all his Formalities, lighting all the Lamps of the Altar, perfumes the Bread with Incenſe, and cuts it into pieces as ſmall as a Grain of Wheat. Then being put up in a certain Veſſel, it is laid up for all occaſions of the Sick for that year. When any is Sick, he takes one of theſe Grains of Bread, and putting it into the Chalice, he carries it in his hand to the Sick Man's Houſe: All that meet him by the way, go back with him to the ſick Man's Houſe: But at *Conſtantinople*, and other Cities where the *Turks* are numerous, the Prieſt carries it ſecretly under his Arm, for fear of ſome affront.

The Prieſt is oblig'd to carry this Sacrament to thoſe that have the Plague, in which caſe, he puts the Grain of Bread into a Raiſon, and gives it him at the end of a long Cane. When

When any person (*a*)dyes, a Lamp is lighted over the Corps, and the House is perfum'd with Incense. Then the Corps being stript, they dip a Sponge or Lint in warm Water, and draw it over the Face, Knees, and Feet, in form of a Cross: Then taking a white Linnen Cloth, they make a Hole in the middle, large enough for the Head to come out, and sewing it up close at the Feet, they cloath him again with the best Garments the Party Deceased had. When the Corps are ready to go to Church, the Priest goes before the Corps with a Cross and a Taper in his hand, singing certain Prayers. At the Church, the Office for the Dead being ended, the Friends and Kindred of the Party Deceased, come and kiss the Corps. The Corps being brought to the Grave, the Priest takes some of the Earth, and sprinkling upon the Head, and the Feet, and the two Sides, in form of a Cross, saying these words:

(*a*) *Burial of the dead.*

The Earth is the Lords, and the fulness thereof; Take O Earth, that which is form'd of thee by the hand of God, who hath received that which was made according to his likeness, and do thou take the Body which belongs to thee.

Then the Priest throws upon the Corps some Water, or Oyl, out of one of the Church-Lamps, and a piece of flaming Incense, and so the Corps are covered. In *Samos* they give Bread and Wine at the Church, to those that accompany the Corps to Church.

Three days after Interment, the Friends of the (*a*) Deceased have a solemn Office at the Church for the Dead. After the Office is ended, they have a sort of small Junket, which they distribute, and Eat in the Church, with Wine, or Strong Water, to wash it down. This sort of Junket they call Κολυβα, *Colyba*, and they derive its first Institution from the time of *Julian* the Apostate, who to spite

(*a*) Commemoration for the Dead.

the Isle of SAMOS.

spite the *Christians*, commanded all the Bakers to raise their Paste with the Blood of Beasts that were Sacrific'd to Idols. The *Christians*, ignorant of the command, were about to buy the Bread, till St. *Theron*, that was a Martyr under *Maximin*, appearing to the Patriarch *Eudoxius*, admonish'd him to forbid the *Greeks* to Eat any Bread of the Bakers making, because it was mix'd with the Blood of Beasts offer'd to Idols. The Patriarch then ask'd the Saint what the People should Eat. He told them *Colyba*, and so shew'd him the way how to make it. But now the *Greeks* use it at these Funeral Commemorations, and on a *Shrove-Sunday*; and the Sunday before *Pentecost*.

Moreover they have another Commemoration for the Dead, nine dayes after Burial, at the House where the Party dy'd. Then again forty days; then at the end of three Months; then of six Months; then of nine Months, and at laſt of twelve Months. The firſt Year of the party Deceaſed being expired, the Commemoration is only Annual.

Every Pariſh hath an anniverſary Feaſt, in Commemoration of that peculiar Saint or Patron, to whoſe memory that Church is Dedicated, and by whoſe name it is called. All they of the Pariſh, and others that have a particular devotion for the Saint, carry with them a preſent of Bread, of a Wax-Taper and Frankincenſe. The Bread goes to the Arch-Biſhops Vicar General; the Tapers and Incenſe to the ſervice of the Church.

And now we have finiſhed the Deſcription of *Samos*, and the ſtory of its preſent State and Condition, by which one place being one of the largeſt of the *Archipelago* for Circumference, and one of the Fruitfulleſt for Soil, We may gueſs at the condition of all the reſt that are rich enough to maintain a Turkiſh Governour.

Beſides

the Isle of SAMOS.

Besides it acquaints us in great part with the Religion of the whole *Greek* Church, which throughout the whole extent of the Patriarch of *Constantinoples* Jurisdiction, is very uniform, without any variation of Rites or Ceremonies.

A

A DESCRIPTION

Of the ISLE of

Nicaria, olim Icarus.

THe Isle of *Nicaria* being under the Jurisdiction of the Arch-Bishop of *Samos*, I thought it expedient to add this Relation of it, as a Supplement to that of *Samos*.

Nicaria lies in length East and West; its prospect on the North is to *Scio*, on the South to *Paros* and *Naxos*, on the East to *Patmos*, and the West to *Mycone*. Three Miles distant from the Island, on the South-side towards *Patmos*, lye some small Islands unhabited; but known by the name of *Furny*, and furnish'd with good Harbours, capacious enough for all sorts of
Ves-

the Isle of NICARIA.

Vessels. Here the *Corsairs* of *Malta*, and other *Christians*, us'd to lay in wait for Ships that trade from *Scio* to *Rhodes*. It lies twelve Miles distant from *Samos*. The Sea about it was formerly call'd the *Icarian* Sea, from *Icarus*, so Famous among the Ancient Poets.

Quid fuit ut tutas agitaret Dædalus
 alas,
 Icarus *immensas nomine signet*
  aquas?
Tot premor adversis, ut si comprendere
 coner
 Icariæ *numerum dicere coner aquæ.*
  Ov. l. 4. El. tr. 5.
Icarus Icariis *nomina fecit aquis.*
Transit & Icarium, *lapsas ubi perdidit alas*
 Icarus, *& vastæ nomina fecit aquæ.*
  Ovid. l. 4. Fast.

It is upwards of fourscore Miles in compass, and yet has not one Port nor Road for great Ships, but only two small Creeks for little Boats. The one called τὸν ἅγιον φῶκα,

Φῶκα, *Ton Hagion Phoca*, from a Church here dedicated to St. *Phocas*: The other is called *Keramy*, so extremely bad, that they that come a shore here are forc'd to draw up their Boats after them. A Mile of *Keramy* is a little Island call'd Καραβοςάσι, *Karavostasi*, or the Rode for small Vessels, call'd *Karavia*. This affords a good retreat for Vessels in Tempestuous Weather. And when 'tis fair, they lade and unlade their Vessels with all possible speed, at the Shore of *Icarus*, and so retire, for fear of a Storm.

(a) Hor. od. 7. l. 3. *Scopulis surdior Icari.*

All the (a) Island is very Mountainous and full of Rocks, which causes but few Villages, and those very small, none of them exceeding an 100 Houses. The Promontory towards *Samos* is call'd *Phanari*, or the *Lanthorn*; because of a Watch Tower here built, to give light to Marriners in the Night. The Tower is yet standing, and the common People are so far mistaken in the common Fable, as to pretend that *Icarus* and his Son were

were here kept Prisoners. But they are given to a Credulity of new reports more inconvenient than that of old Fables, and that the belief of Treasures hid in all old Ruins ever since the taking of *Constantinople*, where so much was found long after it was burn'd. This conceit blown up by various reports, and the Itch of talking on one side, and the great credulity of ignorant People on the other, hath encreased into a vulgar Tradition, very incommodious to the *Greeks*, and whereat the *Turks* take great advantage against them, in case they meddle with any Ruins, either for Curiosity or Use. And And these Islanders have a common Tradition, that about this old Tower of *Icarus* lyes a great treasure, whereof part, though not all, they say, was carri'd away some 40 years ago, by some *Asiaticks*, that came over by stealth, and in the Night, dug up all the ground; And an old Man, whom I spoke with, that saw them at work, but durst not come neer

till

till they had all gone aboard, and set Sail, upon his approach, found the dead Carkase of a Man newly slain; whom they suppose was sacrific'd to the Genius of the place, or the Guardian Angel of the Treasure. They add besides, that before this adventure of the *Asiaticks*, the place was haunted with a Spirit, which alwaies appear'd in black, and destroy'd their Oxen, at least one in a year. But since that time, the place was no more haunted, nor did the Labourers ever complain of the loss of an Ox.

About this Shore are the best Cockles of all the *Archipelago*. The principal Villages are 1. *Cachoria*, of 100 Houses, and two or three *Ches*. 2. *Steli*, famous for great abundance of Nut-Trees. 3. *Musara*, besides which is an Hermitage, and a Church, wherein are kept the Reliques of St. *Theoctistes*, who was of *Lesbos*, and whom the People do think yet does Miracles at this day. Here are in the Isle, the Ruins of a greater Town

Town than any now is. The Church is yet standing, and goes by the name of St. *Hellens*. The Beauty of its Fabrick, is a clear argument, it was built in the days of the *Constantinopolitan* Emperours; and though it has no House neer hand it, yet great resort is made hither for Devotion; and from time to time there never wants a *Papas* to say the Prayers of the Church in it.

There are besides these three already nam'd, a great many little Villages scatter'd up and down through the whole Island, which for the number of Houses, are larger of extent than those in *Samos*; for here every House is environ'd with its proper Garden, Orchard; but the Houses in *Samos* are commonly built closer, and their Gardens, and Orchards at a greater distance.

The whole Island is for the most part Mountainous, and Rocky. The Valleys are few, and little in compass; so that with great labour, and

and difficulty, they force out of so barren a Soil, that little Corn they have; which is not sufficient to feed the Inhabitants above one half the year; and lays a necessity upon the *Nicarians* to traffick abroad for supplies elsewhere. But principally they trade to *Scio* for Corn, whither they carry Wood from *Samos*, and the neighbouring parts of *Natolia*. They are very expert in making Boats, and small Vessels, which are in such esteem, that they are bought up by all their Neighbours. Besides their Traffick in Wood and small Vessels, they vend good store of Sheep and Goats, wherewith their Mountains are well stor'd. And yet their care to keep them is so small, that without either milking them, or driving them into Coats, or Folds, or making any limits or bounds, they only visit them twice a Year, to count the number of their Flocks, and to imprint the Marks of the proper Owners. Some there are, and those of the Richest,

Richeſt, that are at the trouble of milking ſo many, as may ſupply their Family with Cheeſe. They vend likewiſe good ſtore of Swines Fleſh. Wax, and Honey they have great plenty of, but their Honey is in no great eſteem, becauſe of that bitterneſs of taſte which it receives from their Bees feeding upon Firr leaves, which Tree that Iſland abounds with.

The moſt commendable thing of this Iſland is their Air and Water, both ſo healthful, that the People are very long liv'd, it being an ordinary thing to ſee perſons in it of an 100 years of Age, which is a great wonder, conſidering how hardily they live. There is not a Bed in the Iſland, the Ground is their Tick, and the cold Stone their Pillow, and the Cloaths they wear is all the Coverlet they uſe. They provide no more Apparel than what they wear all at once, when that is paſt wearing any longer, then think of a new Suit. Betwixt their ordinary times of
Eating,

Eating, there is not a piece of Bread to be found in the Isle. A little before Dinner, they take as much Corn as will serve that Meal, grind it with a Hand-Mill, bake it upon a flat Stone; when 'tis Bak'd, the Master of the Family divides it equally among the Family; but a Woman with child has two shares. If any Stranger comes in, every one parts with a Piece of his own share to accommodate the Stranger. Their Wine is always made with a third part Water, and so very weak and small. When they drink it, so much as is thought sufficient is put into one large Bowl, and so passes round. The *Nicarians* are the only Islanders of all the *Archipelago*, that neither keep Wine to sell, nor lay it up in Wooden Vessels, but in long Jars, cover'd all over in the Ground. When they have a mind to Tap it, they make a Bung-hole in the top, and draw it out with Canes. Their Houses are so plain, that all the Furniture you can see is an

Hand-

the Isle of NICARIA.

Hand-Mill, besides this, there is nothing but bare Walls: That little they have besides is all hid under Ground; not so much for fear of the *Corsairs* (from whom their Poverty is a sure guard) as out of Custome. Nor are they all so poor, as not to be able to buy Beds, but custom has brought them into a contempt of Beds, as meerly superfluous; insomuch, that when they Travel into other Islands, they refuse the offer of a Bed. A Priest of *Nicaria* coming into *Samos*, was courteously entertain'd by those of his Order, and at Night was offer'd a Bed to lye in; he thank'd them, but refus'd, nor could by any importunity be prevail'd upon, but told them the Earth was his Mother, from whence he would not keep a distance; besides he was afraid of being Sick, if he should lye in a Bed; and therefore if they had a kindness for him, they must give him the liberty of sleeping after his own Country way.

When I went to visit them as Arch-

Arch-Bishop, and ignorant of the custom of the Country, carry'd no Bed. At Night, where I first lodg'd, asking for a Chamber, they told me they had no other than that where I first came; then asking for a Bed, they told me it was not the Custom of the Country; then desiring to borrow some Bed Cloaths for Love or Money, all they brought me was one Smock made of course Dimity.

They have no great communication one with another, any farther than the publick times of Sacred Solemnities, or Civil Business doth cause them to come together. At other times they keep strictly within the narrow Sphere of their own affairs. Formal Visits, Treats, and Entertainments, are things unknown. If any business do put them upon a Visit to their Neighbour, they come not close to his Door, but stand off at a great distance, and call aloud to him; If he make them answer, they discourse the Business they came about,
standing

standing off at the same distance; except they be earnestly invited to come in. And this way of discoursing at a distance they practice more in the Fields and Mountains; their Voices being so strong, that 'tis ordinary to talk at a Miles distance; sometimes at four or five, where the Valleys interpos'd between two hills, give advantage to the Voice. Sometimes they can discourse at that distance, that the carriage of the Sound through the Winding of the Valleys, shall require half a Quarter of an Hours time; and yet they make distinct, and proper Answers, both audible and intelligible, without the help of a *Stentorophonical* Trumpet.

Their Habit for the Men, is a Shirt, and over it a short Cassock, down to the Knees, to which, in Winter they add only a short Vest, that reaches a little below the middle. Stockings they never wear. There Shoes are only a piece of thin Copper, bow'd to the shape of their Feet, and every one is his own

own Shoe-maker. The Women have nothing but one Smock, but so large, that they wrap it double, or treble down to the Girdle, but below the Girdle single. The Priests, for greater reverence in the Church, ty two Towels about their Legs, the one is their usual Bonnet, and the other their Girdle: so that they perform sacred Offices unguirt, as well as uncover'd.

Of all the Isles of the *Archipelago*, this only admits of no mixture with strangers in Marriage, nor admits any stranger to settle with them: They being, as they pretend, all descended of the Imperial Blood of the *Porphyrogenneti*, must not stain their noble Blood with inferiour Matches, or mixtures with *Choriats*, or Peasants, for so they term all the other Islanders.

Porphyrogenneti, were those of the Blood Royal, in the Days of the *Greek* Emperours, so call'd; from their wearing of Purple, which was a Badge of Royalty, and allow'd only to Princes of the Blood;

Blood; and not from an houſe call'd *Porphyra*, where the Empreſſes were wont to *lie in*. But Purple was throughout the Eaſt, the known Badge of Royalty. Hence came that unſanctify'd Wit, and learned'ſt Writer that ever oppos'd the *Chriſtian* Religion with his Pen, to be call'd *Porphyrius*: For his true name in the Language of *Syria*, his native Country, was *Malchus*, or King; but the *Greeks* did paraphraſe it *Porphyrius*, or Purple-robed; that being a Colour peculiar to Kings.

They have a great Happineſs, by reaſon of their poverty, in not being moleſted by the *Turks*, who think it not worth their while to come among them, nor if they ſhould, were they likely to enjoy any quiet, without keeping a ſtronger Guard than the Revenues of the Iſle would maintain. Once they ſlew a *Caddee*, ſent by the Grand Signior, and being ſummon'd to Anſwer for their Crime, they by common conſent own'd the Fact;

but

but would name no particular Man. So that the *Turkish* Officers looking upon their beggerly Cloaths, thought there was neither gain nor glory in punishing such Miscreants, and that in Justice, they must punish all, or none, dismiss'd them untouch'd. From that time no *Turk* ever troubled them: For they take all courses imaginable to seem poor; and wheresoever they come abroad, they count it no shame to beg Alms: Yet they make a shift every year to levy 300 Crowns for the Arch-Bishop. They are govern'd by a *Proesti* of their own chusing, who also levys their Haratch or Tribute to the Grand Signior, and takes care to carry it to the *Aga* of *Scio*. As for their Religion, it is the same with that of *Samos*; but their Priests are more ignorant.

Thus you have an account of a small Island, the Poorest, and yet the Happiest of the whole *Ægean* Sea. The Soil is Barren, but the Air is Healthful; their Wealth is
but

but small; but their Liberty and Security is great. They are not molested with the Tyrannous Insolence of a *Turkish* Officer, nor with the frightful Incursions of barbarous and merciless Pirates. Their Diet and Apparel is below the Rate of Beggars in other Countrys, and their Lodging is a thing of no more care, or cost, than that of the Beasts of the Field, yet their Bodies are strong and hardy, and the People generally long liv'd. They live with as little forecast, as if they expected not to survive a Day, being contented to satisfy the present necessities of Nature. They do properly *In diem vivere*, or as we say, From Hand to Mouth. They have but little, yet they never Want. Their Ignorance is equal to their Poverty, and contributes much to their content. And how well they esteem of their own condition, their contempt of their Neighbouring Islands, and scorning to mix with them in Alliance by Marriage, is a manifeſt ſign. Whence we may learn, that they approach the neareſt to Contentedneſs is this Life; whoſe deſires are contracted into the narroweſt compaſs.

A

DESCRIPTION

Of the ISLE of

PATMOS.

THE Isle of *Patmos*, now call'd *Patino*, is 36 Miles in compass, 40 Miles from the Continent of *Asia*, towards *Ephesus*; as many Miles distant from *Samos* North East of it; 30 from *Nicaria*, North; 60 from *Paros*, and *Naxos*, West; 60 from *Amurgos*, South.

The Figure is neither round nor square, but irregular, by reason of unequal Promontories and Bays. It is furnish'd with very commodious Havens, to which it owes its being inhabited, though not so well as in former times, as appears by the many and great Ruins in it.

This Island was eminent for those wonderful Revelations which the Blessed Apostle, and Evangelist St. *John* had in it, during his banishment thither in the time of the Persecution under *Domitian*. The substance of what is related in that Life of St. *John*, that goes under the Name of *Prochorus*, is generally believ'd in *Patmos* to this day. And though the Author might be of later years than *Prochorus*, the Disciple of St. *John*, as the most judicious Historians of later days do pronounce him to be: Yet that the whole contents of that Book should be a meer Fable, and nothing but the Product of the Authors invention and fancy, is very improbable. For though he might take great liberty in the Manner and Circumstance of what he relates, yet the Matter and Substance were built upon some foundations of real Truth, and such as many Books now not extant, and the Streams of Tradition then nearer the Fountain, but now run dry, might acquaint

quaint him with. That the Island, at St. *John*'s first coming were all Idolaters, had people possessed with Devils, and were mis-led with Magicians, is more than probable, That St. *John*'s casting a Devil out of young *Apollonides*, had a great influence on the peoples Conversion, and rais'd him the Enmity of a Magician, and all that he could draw after him, is a thing reasonably credible. The Name of *Cynops* the Magitian, is known to all the People to this day; yea, not without some very improbable circumstances of the Story, that St. *John* should cause him to jump twice into the Sea, and the second time to be turn'd into a Rock, which now bears his name. However it is no small credit to a Place, otherwise very inconsiderable, that that great Apostle, once the peculiarly beloved Disciple; who of all the Apostles, did alone survive our Saviours judicial coming into his Kingdom of Power and Vengeance upon the *Jewish* Nation: that he should

should be for no small time an Inhabitant of this Island, and there Pen that Mysterious and Sublime Book, which to him indeed was *Apocalypse*, but to all others *Apocrypha*, to him a Revelation, but to us yet an hidden Mystery: like the former Prophecies of the Old Testament, that were never rightly understood till actually fulfill'd. The Tradition of this Island is very positive, that he writ his Gospel here likewise, and that upon the Request of the Islanders, who at his departure, after seven years abode in the Island, did importune him to leave them in writing what they ought to believe: Whereupon he staid eight days longer, to dictate the Gospel to his Disciples that writ it.

They add more, that as he was beginning the Work, there happned a great Thunder and Earthquake, whereupon, looking up to Heaven, he spake those words; Ἐν ἀρχῇ ἦν ὁ λόγος : *In the beginning was the word.* Besides, it is a most
confirm'd

the Isle of PATMOS.

confirm'd Tradition, that the Cavern, which now goes by the name of the Holy *Grotto*, was made by the Rupture of the Earth, in that Earthquake.

The Original of this Island, as it is at this day, is ascribed to St. *Christodoulus*, in the Days of *Alexius Comnenus*.

It was *Alexius Comnenus*, the first of that name, in whose dayes began the Holy War, who reigned the 20 last years of the tenth Century, and the 18 first of the eleventh, and was contemporary with *William* the Conquerour, and *Godfrey* of *Bulloigne*. This *Christodoulus* was Abbot of *Latros*, and had jurisdiction over some 20 Monasteries in *Asia*, near a great Lake about a days Journey and half from *Ephesus*. He being molested by the *Turks*, (whose power now mightily encreas'd in *Asia*) obtained leave of the Emperour to build a Monastry in *Patmos*: Whither having transported his Wealth and Family, he built a Monastry near the Port
of

of *Neſtia*, and named it *Rouvali*. But not liking the place, (and as the Tradition goes, being warned by a Viſion, and a Voice from Heaven,) he quitted that Monaſtry, and built another in the higheſt part of the Iſland, and fortifi'd it with a ſtrong Caſtle, environ'd with high and ſtrong Walls: And there he built a Church. The Inhabitants that lay ſcatter'd in the Iſle, deſired leave to build Huts neer the Monaſtry, for their better Shelter, and defence, in caſe of any ſudden Attaque by Pirats. In proceſs of time, theſe Huts were chang'd into fair Houſes, and by Trade and Commerce, became a great Town, to the number of 800 Houſes, and there Inhabited by rich Merchants, that traded into all parts. But the many Revolutions that have happen'd ſince, have eclips'd the former Glory of the place: And their Ships of Merchandiſe are all dwindl'd into ſmall Fiſher Boats, and the Inhabitants are all extremely poor.

About

About half a mile from this place ſtands the Holy *Grotto*, where St. *John* the Evangeliſt is ſaid to have writ the *Apocalypſe*. Here is a ſmall Monaſtry, under the Juriſdiction of a *Caloir*. The Inhabitants of the neighbouring Borough, pay great Devotion to this place. They talk here of a Fig-Tree, whoſe Figs have naturally the Characters of the Word Αποκάλυψις. *Apocalypſis*. Near the *Grotto* is a ſtone Font, where St. *John* the Evangeliſt is ſaid to have baptiz'd.

The beſt Port of this Iſland, and of all the *Archipelago*, on the Weſt ſide towards *Naxos*, is call'd *Scala*, or the *Wharf*, becauſe of a Wharf built of ſtone for the convenient lading or un-lading of Ships. That which renders it free from annoyance of Winds are certain little Iſlands that ſhelter it from the Eaſt and North-eaſt Winds. The *Venetian* Fleet were wont to winter here during the War of *Candy*.

Beſides this Port, ſtands an entire Village, call'd *Phocas*, without an Inhabitant.

Inhabitant. Here is likewise among old Ruins, a Church yet standing, which they say was built in St. *John*'s days, and they shew something like a Pulpit, where they say St. *John* us'd to Preach. 2. *Merike*, whose neighbouring Hills are well stored with Vine-yards. 3. *Leukes*, fortify'd with a Castle for the Retreat of the Labourers in the Vine-yards, and well supply'd with fresh Fish, from a neighbouring Lake. 4. *Myrsini*, from the growth of Myrtles hereabouts. Here is a Fountain of excellent Water, which the People call Ἁγίασμα, *Hagiasma*, or *Holy-Well*. 5. St. *Nicholas*, from a Church here dedicated to that Saint. 6. St. *George*'s from a Church here dedicated to that Saint: This is a convenient place for Ships to take in fresh Water at. Two Miles hence are the Ruins of an old Town call'd Πλάτυς αἰγιαλος, *Platys Gialos*, or the *Broad shore*; but now it is cover'd with the shrub *Arbutus*, which the *Greeks* call *Coumara*, in old

Greek

Greek Κωμαρον: it bears a Fruit like a Strawberry, but much bigger. 7. *Turcolimnionos*, or the *Turks* Port, because it is frequented by the *Corsairs*. Betwixt this place and Port *Scala*, a rich Merchant *Nicholas Mathas* did lately build a Tower at *Livadi* ; it being a convenient place for Vine-yards and Fishing. 8. *Agrio Livadi*, before which lies St. *Thecla*'s Isle with a little Church, dedicated to that Saint. 9. Port *Sapsila*, before which lies a little Island, with a Church in it, dedicated to St. *Luke*. 10. Port *Gricou*, next to *Scala* for commodiousness. The Island *Tragonesi*, or Isle of *Goats*, defends it from all Winds. 11. *Diacopti*, famous for Salt Pits, which belong to the *Caloirs*. Besides this Port, is a steep Rock of a very great height, which they call *Cynops*, from the Magician in St. *John*'s days, whom the People report to have lodg'd in a great Cave in this Rock ; which Cave they yet believe to be haunted by Devils. For once letting down a Man

Man into't by a Cord for curiosity; to see what was in the Cave, they pull'd him up dead. 12. *Meloi*, a Mile from Port *Scala*. And so we have finish'd the Circuit of the Island, in naming the Ports.

The Inland Villages are 1. *Livadi*. 2. *Vagie*, well beset with Vines and Figtrees. 3. *Megalocampos*, rich in the same Fruits, and accommodated with a Lake well stor'd with Fish. 4. *Hagio Theophanes*, from a Church there dedicated to that Saint, and built by St. *Christodoulos*. 5. *Sazousa*, close by the Sea, near to which are hot Springs of Water, that cure many Diseases. The Island is well stored with Vines, Figg-Trees, Lemon and Orange Trees; and Corn sufficient for the Inhabitants, if they could keep what they have free from the Robbery of Pirats, as well *Christian* as *Mahometan*, that often pillage the poor People, who have no other remedy but patience, and sometimes the pleasure of seeing them perish at Sea, that have been

so

the Isle of PATMOS.

so injurious to a Shore. The *Patmians* complain more of the Cruelty of the *Christian* Pirats, than of the *Turks*. And though the Islanders have procur'd Charters and Patents from the Pope; the King of *France*; from the State of *Venice*; from the Dukes of *Tuscany*; from the Grand Master of *Maltha*, to secure them from the Injuries of *Christian Corsairs*; it is so far from prevailing upon them to withhold their hands from rapine, that it does but provoke them to more fierceness. Yet these Pirats sometimes are made the visible objects of Divine Vengeance. About six years ago, the Marquess de *Fleury*, that carry'd away not only the Grazing, but the Working Cattle, had got no further than *Paros*, 'till his Ship sunk in the Port, and he was taken Prisoner, and clapt into custody at *Corfou*, by the *Venetians*. Another that pillag'd the Monastry of *Liptos*, had no sooner put to Sea, but meeting with some *Saiks*, to which he gave earnest Chase, he run himself a Ground, and there perish'd he, and all his Company.

Let us now return to the State and Government of the Place. The whole Island was given by *(a) Alexius Comnenus*, to *Christodoulus*, and his successours in the Monastry, and the Islands near about, that were not inhabited. And what Culture they bestow on the little Islands, or what Cattle they put to Grazing there, becomes all a Prey to the *Corsairs*; so that the Revenues of this Monastry are now much diminish'd, and the Monks become extremely poor. And his Son *Calo Johannes*, gave also fourteen Villages in *Candie*: But the *Turks* left them but one small Hospital in *Candie*, which yields them 200 Dollars a Year, whereas their Revenues before were at least 13000. Besides the great Monastry, there is a little Nunnery, containing 40 Nuns. This was built but an age ago. They purchase their living by their labour, for they have no Revenues; only the Abbot of the great Monastry

Circiter annum Christi 1100.

ſtry is oblig'd to ſupply them with a Reverend Ancient Monk, to do all Sacred Offices among them. Beſides theſe, there are ſome ſmall Hermitages that maintain ſome few Monks. 1. The Hermitage of the Holy *Grotto* of St. *John* the Divine. 2. The Hermitage of the *Paraſceve*. 3. Of the Annuntiation of the Bleſſed Virgin, lately built by a Biſhop in this laſt Century. 4. The Hermitage, called *Aſomati*. Laſtly, in a place called the Gardens, which furniſh the Monks Kitchin with all neceſſaries. They have certain Chappels conſecrated for the Labourers, at certain Hours, to hear Prayers, and ſo return to their Work.

And this is the preſent Condition of the Iſle of *Patmos*, once famous for the Reſidence of that great Apoſtle St. *John*, and for the great and myſterious Revelation he had in it. But now groaning under the Yoke of ſuch Lords as are common enemies to the Chriſtian Faith, by whom they are both kept in great awe, and slavish obedience, and yet ill protected against the violent Incursion of Pirats and Robbers: so that Poverty is their best Protection against Rapine, and Patience the only Remedy against the grievous Yoak of Tyrannical Oppression.

A

A DESCRIPTION OF MOUNT *ATHOS*.

Mount *Athos* is a demy-Isle, or Chersonese, lying betwixt the Gulf of *Strymon*, from a River of that name on the North, and the Gulf of *Singus*, from the Town *Singus*, on the South. The *Isthmus*, or Neck of Land that parts them, is not much above a Mile broad: It is called by the *Greeks* Ἅγιον ὄρος, and *Athonas*, by the *Franks*, (or Western *Christians*) *Monte Santo*. It is 170 Miles in compass. *Lemnos* stands directly East of it, some 40 Miles distant, and a little before Sun-set is overshadow'd by it. *Thassos* is 30 Miles distant to the

North-east. *Thessalonica* is four days Journey to the West, and *Philippopoli* as many to the North. On the Land side there stands erected a great Wooden Cross, beyond which all Women are forbidden to pass. Because the *Caloirs*, the only Inhabitants of the place, are forbidden all communication with Women, as the principal Rule of their Profession.

Not far from this Cross, without the Bounds, on the Water-side, stands a Village call'd *Alladiava*. The Inhabitants live most upon Fishing, and bring their Fish to sell to the *Caloirs*. If perchance their Wives, or any Women of their Family come along with the Men, they are left in the Boat, and not suffer'd to step a Shore, for fear of Excommunication; for the highest Rule of Discipline, and the most strictly observed, is that of not conversing with Women. And for more caution, and better security of preserving this Rule inviolable, they suffer no other Female

Female Creature of what kind foever, nor any Children, or young men, that are Beardless to come within the Mount.

In describing the place, we cannot pass from Town to Village, but only from Monastrys to Hermitages.

1. The first, and most ancient, (*a*) St. *Laura*, built by *Athanasius*, who obtained special Licenfe of the Emperour of *Constantinople* to retire hither, and found a College of Monks; so called, from that Monastry of *Laura* of *Bethlehem*, where St. *Saba* liv'd, and his Disciple *John*, once Bishop of *Colonia* in *Armenia*, and afterwards Monk, after the Discipline of St. *Saba*; whose Disciples, from a peculiar Rule of Silence, which they did folemnly profess, and strictly practice, were call'd *Silentiarii*. Of this Order was *Anastasius* the Emperour, before he was advanc'd to the Imperial Dignity: Of whom *Baronius* relates, that in the Year of our Lord, 491, he was from a

(a) *Saint Laura's Monastry.*

Professour of silence, made a Soveraign Prince; *Ex Silentiario factus Imperator.* The Monks of the place have a long Story, how this *Athanasius*, wanting Money to go on with the great Church of the Monastry, which he had begun, was met with by the Blessed Virgin, who took his staff from him, and smote a Rock, till it sent out a Spring of Water, that runs at this day; then thrusting his staff into the Ground, it became a Tree, and sent forth Boughs and Leaves. Then she bid him take no care for necessaries, she would provide, and did avow her self to be the Patroness of that Monastry, and of the whole Mountain. This Monastry is about a Mile from the Sea, on the East side, and hath a convenient Channel, that brings up Vessels to their very Walls; where they have a strong Magazin, and a Sentinel perpetually standing to give notice of any *Corsairs*. It hath likewise a very fair Church, and in their Hall, where they eat in common,

common, there is a large Marble Table, where 600 Monks sit down together.

2. The Monastry of (a) *Caracale*, the Name of its Founder, who did consecrate it to the Apostles St. *Peter* and St. *Paul*. This is eight Miles from the former, towards the North. It maintains 500 Monks. The Gate of the Monastry is adorn'd with an exceeding high Tower. Here is likewise a Cistern cut out of a Rock 26 Fathoms deep. This also being near the Sea, has upon the shore a Watch Tower, a Magazin, and a little Port.

(a) *Caracale.*

3. (b) *Philothe*, from the Founders name. This maintains but 50 Monks, though well stor'd with Orchards and Gardens, with its Watch Tower, and Magazin also by the Sea side. Their Church is dedicated to the Annuntiation of the Blessed Virgin.

(b) *Philothe.*

4. (c) *Imberus*; by the name of its Founder. This Monastry is in great repute for a Picture of the Virgin *Mary* upon the Gate, which Picture,

(c) *Imberus.*

Picture, by the report of Tradition, was found floating by the Shore. This Monastry has good Revenues in *Imbrus*, and maintains 400 Monks.

(a) *Coutulmousi,*

5. (a) *Coutulmousi* maintains 300 Monks; it is commodiously surrounded with Gardens, and has a fair Church dedicated to the Transfiguration of our Saviour.

6. *Porpat.* Here is the general Assembly of all the Monastries in this Mountain; hither every Monastry sends a Deputy under the name of *Proesti*, whose business is to reside in the place, and to be ready to consult of all affairs that concern the publick Good. Here is every *Saturday* a publick Market, and the only Market within the whole circumference of the Mount. Here also dwells the *Aga*, with two or three other *Turks*, who protects them from all injuries of other *Turks*, especially of the Sea-men from *Barbary*, whom they call *Levents*. The *Bostangy-Basha* appoints this Officer from amongst the *Bostangies*.

stangies. He is to stay in his Office two years, and then another succeeds him. He is maintained at the common charge of the *Caloirs*, who give him a yearly Pension. And besides, upon every Church Festival, he is invited from Monastry to Monastry, by course, and there, besides the Entertainment of him and his Retinue, he is always presented with a Purse of Money, according to the abilities of the Monastry.

7. *Stauro-Nikita*, or *The Conquering Cross*. This maintains but 30 Monks. Their Church is dedicated to St. *Nicholas*, where they have in great estimation his Picture upon a Board, that was found ready painted, as a Wreck, and devoutly taken up by the Monks of this Covent.

8. *Pantocratoras* maintains 200 Monks; their Church is dedicated to the Transfiguration of our Blessed Saviour.

9. *Vatopedi* maintains 300, their Church is dedicated to the Blessed Virgin. 10. *Tou-*

10. *Toufimenou* has but 80 Monks; the Church is dedicated to the Afcenfion. It is the pooreft of all the Monaftry, not for want of Lands, but of Men to cultivate them. For the foil about, is the beft in all the Mount. It bears Olives of a fingular largenefs, and wants no other fort of Fruit Trees. But the number of the Monks in it amount but to 80, who being not able to make the beft advantage of fo much good ground continue poor in a plentiful Soil.

In the middle of all the Mount ftands 11. *Chiliantary*, a Monaftry of the *Bulgarians*, who fpeak here their own Language, and have their Prayers (though the fame with the *Greek*) in the *Bulgarian* Language. This is the largeft Monaftry of the whole Ifland, and maintains 800 Monks. They have much Land abroad, which they fend their own Monks to cultivate.

12. *Touzographou*, or the *Painters Convent*, from the Founder, who
was

was a Painter. The Church is confecrated to St. *George*, it maintains 200 Monks, all *Bulgarians*. There is a little Church not far from this Monaftry, that ftands alone, and now is ufelefs; but having a fair Picture of St. *George* in it, the Monks thought fit to bring it into their own Church; but to no purpofe, for fo often as they brought it, fo often it takes its leave, and is found the next day in the Church.

13. *Xenophon*, a *Burgarian* Monaftry, has but 30 *Caloirs*.

14. *Caftamoniti* has not above fix, or feven Monks at moft, yet it hath a Chappel dedicated to St. *Steven*.

15. *Archangeli*, which had before another name, but changed to this upon this occafion. A young *Caloir*, that was tilling the Ground abroad, found a Treafure in an old Urn, and brought the news of it to the Superiour of the Convent; he fent with the young Man two other *Caloirs*, who finding the Treafure, agreed between themfelves

selves to kill the Boy, and share it betwixt them; and so they ty'd a Stone about his neck, and cast him into the Sea, and hiding the Treasure, came to the Superiour, and told him the Boy had deceiv'd them, and was run away. Next morning the Sexton found the Boy and the Stone about his neck in the Church, who discover'd all, and told that the Angels *Gabriel* and *Raphael* brought him thither. The two *Caloirs* thus convicted, were banish'd, and this stone set up as a Monument to this day.

16. The Monastry of *Rufficon* has a Church dedicated to *Pantelcimon*, and maintains 20 *Caloirs*.

17. *Xeropotamou*, dedicated to the Memory of 40 Martyrs that were drowned in the Lake of *Sebaste*. This Monastry has 300 Monks, and being by the Sea side, has a Magazin and a great Watch-Tower. Over against this Monastry, on the Continent of *Macedonia*, stands a great Village of Hermits and religious Persons, though
without

Mount ATHOS.

without the bounds of the *Caloirs*.

18. *Simo-Petra*, so called, from the Founder and the Foundation. It is situate on a Rock, and was founded by one *Simon*, an Hermit, who by his Prayers having cured the Daughter of a Governour of *Caſſandria*, did move him to bestow enough for to build this Monastry, and 200 Monks. They shew here an hand for a sacred Relique of St. *Mary Magdalen*'s body, but the Fingers of it are extraordinary great.

19. *Gregorios*, near the Sea, and much infested with Pirats for want of Fortification, and men to defend it, having but 60 Monks.

20. *Dioniſiou*, consecrated to St. *John Baptiſt*, whose Forehead they pretend to shew here as a sacred Relique. Besides they shew the Bones of one *Nymphus*, once Patriarch of *Conſtantinople*, who being weary of publick employment, retir'd hither, unknown to any who he was; so they looking upon him as a poor Vagabond, that wanted work,

work, employ'd him as their Mule-teer, to fetch in their wood; in which employment he continued with great humility and faithfulness many years, not offering to ride any of the Mules going or coming, and kept all the Church Fasts strictly in the midst of all his drudgery. At his death-bed he discover'd to the Superiour who he was, and that he chose that manner of Life to mortifie his proud Flesh: Whereupon, looking upon him as a Saint, they keep his Bones as a sacred Relique.

21. *Hagios Paulos*, so named from the Founder, who was reputed a Saint. It maintains 200 Monks, all *Bulgarians*.

Pass we now to the Hermitages, which are very small, but commonly so neer one another, as to make the appearance of a Village. There are two places where they lye in great numbers. 1. *Hagia Æna*, or St. *Ain*, from a Church dedicated to that Saint. These are the retiring places of such Hermits as live

by

by Manufacture; as particularly, the making of Crosses and Figures that represent our Saviours Passion, and Seals and Marks proper for the consecrated Bread. The *Caloirs* that are sent abroad to confess People, and to gather Alms for pious Uses, buy up all these Manufactures to present unto people among whom they come. These Hermits live more retired and melancholly, being not above two or three, sometimes but one in an House. And they do imitate the Lives of those antient Monks in *Ægypt*, about *Thebais*, that were imitators of St. *Anthony*, who did himself, as did all his followers, live and maintain themselves by hand labour and manufactures, though of a very mean sort, yet enough to earn them Food and Raiment. This St. *Anthony* was the first *Christian* Monk of the World, his Food was only Bread and Water; yet he liv'd 150 years: His fame was so great, that *Helen*, the Mother of *Constantine* the Great, did by letters sent to him, recommend Her self and her Son to his Prayers. He dy'd in the Wilderness. *An. Dom.* 361. 2. *Kerasia*, another plot of Ground, all strew'd with such Hermitages as are at St. *Aine*, and they live in the very same manner.

Besides these Hermitages that lye so neer in voisinage, there are above 1000 more dispersed up and down the Island, which do all belong to some one of the Monastries. If a Man desire to live in a Cell, he gives a certain Rate to that Monastry to which it belongs, and so is empowr'd to enjoy that Cell, and the Land belonging to't for his life: when he dies, it returns to the Monastry, and the Monastry is Heir to all that he leaves behind him. There are Cells of all rates, from 5 Dollers to 150. One thing is very remarkable, that Idleness is utterly banish'd here, no man lives in the Isle, who is not some way employ'd.

As for the maintenance of these Monastries, though their Lands be sufficient to feed them, and their Moun-

Mountain furnish them with Wine enough to drink; yet as the matter is order'd, they commonly want Money to pay their *Haratch*, or yearly Tribute of 3 Dollers *per* Poll, and buy themselves Cloaths and Furniture for tilling their Land. So that every year they select some of their *Caloirs* to go abroad, and beg the Charity of *Christian* People, towards the relief of the respective Monastry. And these are always by two and two together. And the Monastries agree before-hand to what particular places they will send their respective Emissaries, who continue ordinarily two or three years in their perambulation. At their coming home, the Money is delivered to the *Skenaphylax*, or the Steward of the Monastry; for it is against the Rule of their Order, to meddle with Money. He layes it out upon necessary occasions, and what is left, is kept to defray the Charge of another Voyage. They have a Register of those that bestow any thing, and they pray for them

them conſtantly in the Monaſtry.

When they are choſen to go abroad, the Chief of the Monaſtry names one of the *Caloirs* : The Perſon named, in token of his obedience, doth proſtrate himſelf on the Ground before the Superiour of the Monaſtry, and riſing, kiſſes the Superiours hand. Then the Perſon firſt nam'd, names thoſe that ſhall go along with him, who in like obedience, firſt proſtrate themſelves before the Superiour, and kiſs his hand, then do the like to the *Caloir* firſt nam'd by the Convent, and own him for their Father and Superiour, to whom they owe all obedience during their miſſion. When they go abroad, they firſt apply themſelves to the *Metropolite* of the Dioceſe, and ſhew him their Letters of Obedience from their Superiours. Whereupon the *Metropolite* gives them Letters of Permiſſion to ask Charity, and confeſs Penitents throughout his Dioceſe. Where they Confeſs any, they exact nothing of them by way of pecu-
niary

niary Penance; but only receive what in charity they freely bestow.

The beginning of Monks in Mount *Athos*, was from the time that the *Mahometans* invaded *Ægypt* and *Syria*, where the Monks in those places enjoying no security of their lives, came into *Greece*, and desired of the Emperour a Place to live in, according to their Monastick way. He appointed them Mount *Athos*, and *Athanasius* foremention'd, was the first that founded a College here. They professed at first the imitation of St. *Anthony* of *Ægypt*, and St. *Sabas*; but now the Rules of their Order are taken from St. *Basil*.

At their first coming to Mount *Athos*, they were a Colony of the Monks of the *Holy Land*, who follow'd the Rules of St. *Anthony* of *Ægypt*, and St. *Sabas*; but chiefly the Rules of St. *Sabas*, who liv'd long after St. *Anthony*, when Monkery began to alter its mode and fashion, and from a casual Retirement of some few men to a rude and simple way

way of life in the Wilderness, to become subject to Rules and Orders, to incorporate into Societies, to change their Caves into Cloisters, and to remove from Deserts to good dwelling Houses, and places of better convenience and accommodation. This St. *Sabas*, by his eminent and singular strictness, did highly advance the Fame and Admiration of a Monastick life. He was by birth a *Cappadocian*, of the Village of *Mutalasca*, in the Diocese of *Cæsarea*, and being left Heir to a good Estate, under the Care of his Uncle *Hermias*, the perverseness of his Aunt made him quit that Uncles House, and go to *Scandos*, to live with another Uncle, whose name was *Gregory*. This breeding a Dissention between the two Uncles, he, to avoid all occasion of discord, betook himself to the Monastry of *Flaviana* near *Mutalasca*; whence at the eighteenth year of his Age, he went to *Jerusalem*, to visit those places which our Blessed Saviours life and death hath made

so

so memorable. At that time the Fame of *Euthymius*, then Abbot of *Laura* by *Bethlehem*, was very great in the *Holy Land*. This enflam'd young *Sabas* with great desire to be admitted into his Monastry: Wherefore one day as *Euthymius* was going to receive the Sacrament, he fell down at his feet, begging leave to be entred into his College: But *Euthymius* gave him the Repulse, telling him it was not fitting that so young a Man should be admitted into *Laura*; yet he would recommend him to a smaller Monastry hard by, where St. *Theoctistes* was Abbot: Where having stay'd ten years, *Euthymius* admitted him into a Cave by his own Monastry for five years. Then *Euthymius* selected him, and *Domitian* to vye *asketick* Severities in a solitary Place for four years, which having perform'd to great admiration, about the Fortieth year of his Age he retir'd to a Cave by the Brook of *Siloe*. By that time he had liv'd here five years he had a College of Disciples, to the number of 70, amongſt whom was *John* the Silentiary, Biſhop of *Colonia* in *Cappadocia*, before he entred into his Monaſtick life, and afterwards Abbot of this College, which was call'd *Nova Laura*. There were afterwards more Monaſtries of this name in *Palæſtin*. *Laura Pyrgiorum* by *Jordan*, built by one *Jacobus*. *Laura Maliſchæ*, built by *Firminus*, and *Laura Marichæ*, by *Severianus*, and *Laura Elcerebæ*, by *Julianus*. But this *Laura*, built by St. *Sabas*, was the moſt Famous, wherein his life-time the number of his Monks encreas'd to 150. He was eminent in the time of *Anaſtaſius*, *Juſtinus*, and *Juſtinianus*, Emperours of *Conſtantinople*, and dy'd in the 94th year of his Age. His name is yet very remarkable among the Eaſtern *Chriſtians*, eſpecially at Mount *Athos*, whoſe firſt Monks were but a Colony of his Diſciples, and whoſe ancienteſt College is called *Laura*, from his *Laura* in *Palæſtine*.

Their conſtant morning Prayer is three hours before day; their evening

evening Prayer at Sun-set. On *Sundays* they go to Prayers five hours before day in the morning, and before great Holy-days their Prayers continue all night. They have likewise other set hours of Prayer for the day-time.

They that enter into this profession, are kept six months Probationers; during which time they are put to all the Exercise they must undergo in their Profession. After the six months are expired, the Novitiat chuseth among the Old *Caloirs* a God-father to introduce him, and to instruct him in the Ceremony of his Admission. This God-father brings him to the Church door, where he is strip'd to his Shirt, and prostrates himself, then he makes a second prostration in the middle of the Church, and a third at the Altar, and a fourth to the Superiour. Then upon his knees he answers to all the Interrogatories made him by the Superiour, which are commonly these.

Sup. My Brother, what motives have

have you to come to this Altar, and to this Assembly?

Nov. A desire to live a Monastick life.

Sup. Do you come of your free choice, without any constraint?

Nov. Yes.

Sup. Will you for ever stay in the Monastry, and observe its rules?

Nov. Yes.

Sup. Will you keep Chastity, Temperance, and Godliness?

Nov. By the Grace of God.

Sup. Will you all your life be obedient to the Superiour, and his fraternity in Jesus Christ?

Nov. By the Help of God.

After these and some more Questions of like nature, some Prayers are said out of the *Euchologion*, and the Superiour shewing him the Book of the Gospel, doth conjure him by it, if he come to that Profession of his own proper motion. He answering in the Affirmative, the Superiour gives him a pair of Sciffers, bidding him deliver them back into his hand: Which done,
the

the Superiour cuts off a little of his hair in the form of a Cross, saying,

Our Brother N. N. hath his head shaven, in the name of the Father, the Son, and the Holy Ghost. The rest that stand by say three times *Kyrie Eleeson.* Then his Monastick habit is put on in order.

1. his *Cassock*, whereat the Superiour says,

Our Brother N. puts on the Garment of gladness, in the name of the Father, &c. The Company say thrice *Kyrie Eleeson.*

2. His Girdle with these words,

Our Brother girds his reins with the strength of truth, to mortifie his Body, and to renew his Spirit, in the name of the Father, &c. Then follows the *Kyrie Eleeson* thrice.

3. His Bonnet with these words,

Our Brother puts on the Helmet of Hope and Salvation, in the name of the Father, &c.

4. His Mantle, with these words:

He puts on the Mantle as the earnest

earnest of Angelique apparel, and of incorruptible Glory, in the name of the Father, &c.

5. His Sandals, with these words.

He puts on the Shoes of the preparation of the Gospel of Peace, in the name of the Father, &c. with the *Kyrie Eleeson* thrice, as in all the rest. Then after the rehearsal of an Epistle and Gospel, and some Prayers, they put a Cross into his hand with these words:

Our Saviour saith, if any man will be my Disciple, let him deny himself, and take up his Cross, and follow me. Then a Candle lighted is put into his hands, with these words.

Our Lord hath said, Let your Light so shine before men, that they seeing your good works, may glorifie your Father who is in Heaven.

This done, the other *Caloirs*, every one salute him with a Kiss, and so the Ceremony is ended.

The Rules are these,

1. To renounce the World, and
all

all that is near, and dear to them in it, as a Father and Mother, &c. according to that of our Saviour.

2. To continue in the Monaſtry in obedience to the Superiour and his Brethren.

3. To ſuffer all afflictions, and torments for the Love of God.

4. To have nothing of their own, but all in common among their Brethren.

5. To keep themſelves unſpotted from all carnality.

6. To be always ready to go to Prayers at the appointed Hours. At Midnight; before Day; at Noon; at three a Clock after Noon; at Sun-ſet; and after Supper: And after all this, when they go to their Cells, where they lye, to make 60 Proſtrations, which they call *Metánoiá's*, or Pennances, with a ſhort Prayer to every one for the Superiour; for their Brethren; for the Benefactors of the Monaſtry, and in general, for all *Chriſtians*.

7. Not to eat or drink in ſecret; but

but in common with their Brethren; and this is so observ'd, that in case they are pinch'd with thirst betwixt Meals, they drink at the Window, or Door of the Cell, that all may see them, and before they drink, they cry aloud, Ἐυλογεῖ, i. e. *Give thanks.*

8. Not to eat Flesh all their lives, which is so strictly observed in Mount *Athos*, that in no sickness they are permitted to break this rule; but the Monks that Travel, in case of sickness, may eat Flesh, if the Physician advise them to't. But in Mount *Athos* they are allow'd on *Sundays*, *Tuesdays*, *Thursdays*, and *Saturdays*, to eat Eggs, Butter, Cheese, and Fish; the other days they eat none of these, nor drink any thing but Water only; and those other days they have only a Dinner, at Night they eat a piece of Bread, and drink a little water at the Church-door, and so to Prayers, and thence to their Cells, where they remain in great silence. But the Sick, Aged, and

and such as have newly come from a Journey, are allow'd to eat in the common Refectory.

For the better Government of the Monastry, the Superiour goes in person to every man's Cell, accompanied with some of the elder *Caloirs*, and if he find any man out of his Cell, or two or three together in another man's Cell, this is a Crime, after three reproofs very punishable. The younger *Caloirs* stand in great dread of this nocturnal Perambulation, and have that saying of St. *Pauls* very much inculcated. *Heb.* 13. 17.

The Burying of the Dead is much like the way of Burying, described at *Samos*, with this difference, that a Year after Interment, they take up the Scull, and wash it with Wine, and put it in a Charnel, inscribing the name of the Deceased upon the Charnel.

Thus much of Mount *Athos*, wherein is a thing remarkable, beyond all example, that in a space

space of ground, 160 Miles in compass, where no less than 6000 men constantly live, there should not be seen a Woman.

FINIS.

The two Books following are lately Printed for Moses Pitt at the Angel in St. Paul's Church-yard.

THe six Voyages of *John Baptista Tavernier*, Baron of *Aubonne*; through *Turky*, into Persia, and the East-Indies, for the space of forty years. Giving an account of the present State of those Countries, *viz.* of the *Religion, Government, Customs,* and *Commerce* of every Country, and the Figures, Weight, and Value of the Money current all over *Asia:* To which is added the Description of the *Seraglio.* Added likewise a Description of the Countries which Border upon the *Euxine* and *Caspian* Seas: By an *English* Traveller, never before printed. Published by Dr. *Daniel Cox.* 1678. *fol.* price 20 *s.*

Remarks upon the *Manners, Religion,* and *Government* of the *Turks.* Together with a Survey of the Seven Churches of *Asia,* as they now lie in their Ruins: And a Brief Description of *Constantinople.* By *Tho. Smith,* B. D. and fellow of St. *Mary Magdalen* College, *Oxon.* 1678. 8° price 3 *s.*

www.ingramcontent.com/pod-product-compliance
Lightning Source LLC
Chambersburg PA
CBHW021917180426
43199CB00032B/431